The English Moore

Act j. Scene iij.

Arthure : Dionisia

Ar. Deare Sister, beare wth me.
Dio. I may not Brother.
What! Suffer you to pine & weare away,
In yor vnnaturall melancholly fitts:
Wch haue already turnd your pure blood
Into a Toad=poole dye. I am asham'd
(Allmost, vpon my Life) to call you Brother
Ar. O my Sister —
Dio. I can say ô my brother too; to shew you
How ill becomes you (that haue the same cause
Equally wth yor selfe, to spend my Life
In solitary mourning; and would do it,
Could it make good or Losse. My honord father!
A teare has sear'd me there; But that's by the by
And more of Anger 'gainst his Enemy;
And his forever curst Posteritie
That robd vs of a father, then of Sorrow
For what we know is vnrecouerable.
But to sit grieuing ore his memory
In a resolued silence as you doe;
Killing yor owne blood, whilst a vayne holds any
Proceeding from the flesh that drew out his
Is meerly idle. Mingle then yor griefe
Wth thought of braue Reuenge: And doe it not
In priuate meditation in yor Chamber
But beare it out, till it proceed to Action.
Ar. By powring blood on blood.
Dio. By quenching fire of
of high Reuenge wth base vnnaturall blood;
By stopping of our Fathers carelesse wounds,
(Wch still bleed fresh in or best memories)
Wth the proud flesh of him that butcherd his.
Ar. We know he liues not, that has slayne or father:
Or, if he liues, 'tis where I can not reach him.
He neuer saw English harbour, since his sword
Vnfortunately had the better of my father.
Dio. But his sonne liues.
Ar. Good Sister, coole thy passion.
Wth reasonable meanes.
Dio. If you or I
Could wth or Sighes, or teares, blow hence, or wash
Away the memory of a Father; then
I could sit downe by you, & end a Life
As you allmost haue done in pensiuenes
By giuing way to Sorrow. Where's the Spirit
Which my slayne father had? Haue you none of it?
Must I now play the Man; whilst you inherit
Onely my Mothers puling disposition?
Ar. I know thy drift (good Sister Dionisia)
Tis not vnto Reuenge, or blood; but to
Put motion in me, to preuent the daunger
A sad Retirednes might bring vpon mee.
Dio. Bt it as you thinck it, See you walk abroad
And make the house noe longer darck wth Sighing. Ent. Rafe
Now Sr. the newes wth you.
Ra: Newes worth the hearing.

Fol. 4[r] of the presentation copy of Richard Brome's *The English Moore; or, The Mock-Mariage*. Courtesy of the Dean and Chapter of Lichfield Cathedral, Great Britain.

The English Moore; or The Mock-Mariage

by Richard Brome

Edited by Sara Jayne Steen

University of Missouri Press
Columbia, 1983

University of Missouri Press, Columbia, Missouri 65211
Library of Congress Catalog Card Number 83–1095
Printed and bound in the United States of America

Library of Congress Cataloging in Publication Data

Brome, Richard, d. 1652?
The English Moore; or
The Mock-Mariage.

Bibliography: p.
I. Steen, Sara Jayne, 1949– . II. Title.
III. Title: English Moore. PR2439.B5E5 1983 822′.4 83–1095
ISBN 0-8262-0403-1

Acknowledgments

I would like to thank the Dean and Chapter of Lichfield Cathedral for granting me access to, and publication permission for, the manuscript of *The English Moor*; Prebendary E. C. C. Hill, librarian at Lichfield Cathedral, for his generous assistance; Godfrey P. Hives and Lewis Raybould, vergers at Lichfield Cathedral, for their kindness during my stay there; James L. Harner, Bowling Green State University, for his continued guidance and support; Duane Hoynes, Montana State University, for his helpful comments on the text; and Marge Ennes, Montana State University, for typing the manuscript with accuracy and a smile. I would also like to thank the librarians at numerous institutions in England and the United States for their cooperation.

S. J. S.
Bozeman, Montana
May 1983

Contents

Abbreviations

DNB — *Dictionary of National Biography.*

E — Jonson, Ben. *Epicoene.* 1609. In *Ben Jonson*, vol. 5, edited by C. H. Herford and Percy Simpson, 139–272. Oxford: Clarendon Press, 1937.

O — The 1659 octavo of *The English Moor.* When the abbreviation is used, all copies agree.

OED — *Oxford English Dictionary.* The *OED* has been used for denotation, but it is cited only when quoted.

Onions — Onions, C. T. *A Shakespeare Glossary.* 2d ed., rev. 1958. Reprint. Oxford: Clarendon, 1966.

Partridge — Partridge, Eric. *Shakespeare's Bawdy: A Literary & Psychological Essay and a Comprehensive Glossary.* 1948. Reprint. New York: Dutton, 1960.

SD — Stage direction.

Skeat — Skeat, Walter W. *A Glossary of Tudor and Stuart Words, Especially from the Dramatists.* Edited by A. L. Mayhew. 1914. Reprint. New York: Burt Franklin, 1968.

Sugden — Sugden, Edward H. *A Topographical Dictionary to the Works of Shakespeare and His Fellow Dramatists.* Manchester: Manchester University Press, 1925.

TC — Middleton, Thomas, and William Rowley. *The Changeling.* 1622. Reprint. Edited by George Walton Williams. Regents Renaissance Drama Series. Lincoln: University of Nebraska Press, 1966.

TEM — *The English Moor.*

Tilley — Tilley, Morris Palmer. *A Dictionary of the Proverbs in England in the Sixteenth and Seventeenth Centuries: A Collection of the Proverbs Found in English Literature and the Dictionaries of the Period.* Ann Arbor: University of Michigan Press, 1950.

Wright — Wright, Joseph. *The English Dialect Dictionary.* 6 vols. London: Frowde, 1898–1905.

Note on the Text

The entire manuscript text of *The English Moor* is here presented in a semi-diplomatic transcription. The original foliation appears in the right margin and is bracketed so that it won't be confused with the line numbers I added. The letters *r* (recto) and *v* (verso) accompany the manuscript foliation, since there is only one number in the manuscript for both sides of the sheet. The lineation does not vary from the original unless a line does not fit on the page; in this situation, the variation will be obvious because there will be no line number for the overrun. Numeral forms, punctuation, word division, and spelling are retained, including the use of *i* for *j*, the letter *v* for initial *u*, and *u* for medial *v*. I did not reproduce the long *f* or the long *s*, nor did I attempt to approximate the length of dashes, except in cases where the length seems to make a significant semantic difference (for example, in II.iii.101, 112). Decorative signs, which were occasionally used in italic sections in order to fill out lines, are not reproduced, and hyphens, which appear in the manuscript as "-" and as "=" are standardized to current usage ("-"). In cases where it was difficult to determine whether an initial letter was meant to be a miniscule or a majuscule, I relied upon the size of surrounding letters and a knowledge of the usual capitalization practices of the writer and the period. Symbols such as the ampersand are retained. Abbreviations and contractions are not expanded. The spacing in contractions is normalized, as it is often impossible to tell from the handwriting whether, for instance, "to't" or "to 't" was meant; in such cases, the closed form ("to't") is shown. The writer's use of superscript letters is partially standardized, but only in cases where variations of the same word exist in the manuscript (i.e., "w^{ch}," "$w^{c}h$," and "wc^{h}" are always represented as "w^{ch}").

The mixed hand is indicated by roman type, and the italic hand by italic type. In cases where it was difficult to determine whether the writer meant a word to be in mixed hand or fully italic—usually when the writing appears to have been hurried—I followed the writer's usual practice. Interlineations are inserted in the proper lines in the text and are identified in the manuscript notes. When a speaker's name was omitted in the manuscript, or, as is true in a few cases, the speaker was incorrectly identified, the correct name is shown in square brackets in the text, and the addition or alteration is listed in a manuscript note.

Two sets of footnotes appear below the text of the play. Manuscript notes and the few alterations I made—for the sake of clarity or the exigencies of publication—are listed just below the text. The relevant line number and section of text are followed by a closing bracket and an indication of the original manuscript state, as follows:

30 fire] fire of ("of" *deleted*) *MS*.

At line 30, then, the writer of the manuscript wrote "fire of," realized the error, and corrected it by drawing a line through "of" to delete it from the text. Historical and critical notes appear below these manuscript notes, at the bottom of the page. The format is similar to that used with the manuscript notes: the line number and section of text are followed by a closing bracket and a brief explanation or discussion.

The collation for this edition, which is presented in an appendix, is a record of all substantive variants between the manuscript and the 1659 edition of the play (an octavo; see "Printed Texts" in the Introduction for further description of this edition). The collation follows the sequence of the manuscript. After the line number, the manuscript reading is listed first, followed by a closing bracket and the octavo reading, as follows:

58 the] your

A virgule represents a line break for both poetry and prose. When there are several variants in a line, the whole line is collated under a single line number. An ellipsis is used when several intervening words are the same. Lines that are present in the manuscript and not in the octavo are shown as:

101–4 *omit*

Lines from the manuscript that are continued in the octavo on the same line are shown as:

206 [+] Heark thee. *They whisper*

Lines that are present in the octavo and not in the manuscript are shown as:

30 + I'le see it done.

For substitutions, or for lines with so many variants that the normal apparatus is especially cumbersome, the format is:

19–20 *omit*; + But look not after me: I am not mark'd
For Matrimony, I thank my stars.

INTRODUCTION

A Brief Biography of the Playwright

Knowledge of Richard Brome,[1] one of the most popular Caroline playwrights, begins with the Stage-Keeper's line from the Induction to Ben Jonson's *Bartholomew Fair* (1614): "I am looking, lest the *Poet* heare me, or his man, Master *Broome*, behind the Arras."[2] Brome, then, was Jonson's "man" in 1614 and had probably been associated with the famous playwright long enough for his name to have meaning to regular playgoers.[3]

Little is known about Brome's activities during the years preceding and immediately following 1614. His birthdate is generally assumed to be 1590, which would have made him about twenty-four when *Bartholomew Fair* was written. This estimated birthdate corresponds with what is known of his later career. His writing indicates a man of some education—but no more than a bright young man could have picked up from some schooling and from association with Jonson and his circle. In Epigram 101, "Inviting a Friend to Supper," Jonson wrote: "[M]y man / Shall reade a piece of VIRGIL, TACITVS, / LIVIE, or of some better booke to vs."[4] These lines led Ronald Bayne to conjecture that Brome had a grammar-school education and was "not so much a valet as a secretary and amanuensis."[5] It is not certain that the "man" of the undated epigram was Brome, although he may indeed have been able to read Virgil and Livy to Jonson's guests. Brome's subsequent references to himself as an "old serving-creature," however, and the attacks on and defenses of his early lowly status would make no sense had he not held, at least when he began with Jonson, a more menial role.[6]

1. For a more complete discussion of Brome's life, see Catherine Maud Shaw, *Richard Brome*, 17–33; R.J. Kaufmann, *Richard Brome*, 17–34; and Gerald Eades Bentley, *The Jacobean and Caroline Stage* 3:49–92.
2. *Ben Jonson* 6:13.
3. Kaufmann, *Richard Brome*, 19.
4. *Ben Jonson* 8:65.
5. Bayne, "Lesser Jacobean and Caroline Dramatists," 225.
6. "Old serving-creatures oftentimes are fit / T'inform young masters, as in land, in wit" (Brome, "To the Memory of the Deceased, but Ever-Living Author in These his Poems, Master John Fletcher," in *The Works of Beaumont and Fletcher* 1:lxiv). R. Brideoak wrote, in *Jonsonus Virbius* (1638), of the "nasty sweepings of thy servingman" (Clarence E. Andrews, *Richard Brome*, 9). The author of "To the Readers" in the 1659 edition of *Five New Playes* (presumably Alexander Brome) notes that some "think they lessen this *Author's* worth when

Whatever his duties with Jonson might have been, Brome appears to have entered the theatrical world as something more than Jonson's "man" by the early 1620s. In 1623, *A Fault in Friendship* (now lost), written by "*Young* Johnson and Broome," was licensed for Prince Charles's Company.[7] (The identity of "*Young* Johnson" is unknown.) In a 1628 warrant, "Richard Broome" was listed among the Queen of Bohemia's Players.[8] This information raises the question of whether Brome might have been an actor.[9] It would not be surprising if he was—he had a good sense of what was theatrically effective—but no other references exist to his having been an actor, and he might have been included in the warrant because he was writing for the players.[10] Only a year later, on 9 February 1629, his *Lovesick Maid* (also lost) was licensed for the King's Men. The play was "acted with extraordinary applause"; indeed the response was so great that the company presented two pounds, a highly uncommon gift, to the licenser.[11] By this time, Brome was almost certainly no longer in Jonson's employ.

Nor was he in Jonson's favor, at least not for a short time. Brome's *Lovesick Maid* achieved its "extraordinary applause" only a few weeks after Jonson's *New Inn* had failed in the same theater. The older playwright was stung by this turn of events; in an early version of "Ode to Himself," he wrote that audience taste was clearly at a low level and that "Broomes sweeping(s) doe as well / Thear as his Masters Meale."[12] But by the time the poem was published (in 1631), he had reconsidered the sarcastic cut and dropped the reference to Brome. The commendatory verses that he wrote to preface Brome's *Northern Lass* (1632) are warmly dedicated: "To my old Faithfull Seruant: and (by his continu'd Vertue) my louing Friend." In the verses, Jonson praises Brome's skill:

> Now, you are got into a nearer roome,
> Of *Fellowship*, professing my old Arts.
> And you doe doe them well, with good applause,
> Which you haue iustly gained from the *Stage*.[13]

If Brome was hurt by Jonson's sneer, which had circulated, his loyalty to Jonson doesn't seem to have wavered; his references to Jonson are uniformly grateful and admiring.

---

they speak the relation he had to *Ben. Johnson*" and reminds readers that Aesop and Terence were slaves and that Virgil served in a stable (sigs. A4r, A5r–A5v).

7. Joseph Quincy Adams, ed., *The Dramatic Records of Sir Henry Herbert*, 26.

8. Eleanore Boswell and E. K. Chambers, eds., "Dramatic Records," 347.

9. Alwin Thaler, "Was Richard Brome an Actor?"

10. Bentley, *Jacobean and Caroline Stage* 2:389–90.

11. *The Plays and Poems of William Shakespeare*, ed. James Boswell (London, 1821), 1:421, cited in *Dramatic Records of Herbert*, ed. Adams, 32.

12. *Ben Jonson* 6:493; Kaufmann, *Richard Brome*, 24.

13. *Ben Jonson* 8:409.

In the years after *The Lovesick Maid*, Brome's reputation grew. He wrote for the fashionable Blackfriars theater; for the Red Bull, whose acting company was highly reputed at that time; and, beginning in 1635, for Salisbury Court.

His relationship with the Salisbury Court management began amicably, but it became increasingly acrimonious. A Requests Proceedings Bill of Complaint by Salisbury Court against Brome and Brome's response to it, both filed in 1640, provide first-hand knowledge of Brome during the later 1630s.[14] After Brome's *Sparagus Garden* had played at Salisbury Court in 1635 and had made a profit of over a thousand pounds, he signed a three-year contract to write three plays a year in return for fifteen shillings a week and one day's profit from each play. This arrangement worked well until the plague intervened, closing the theaters on 12 May 1636. Both playwrights and companies suffered; Brome's salary was discontinued. He was "*put to* his shifts in that hard sadd and dangerous tyme of the sicknes boeth for himselfe and his famyly,"[15] so he went in August to William Beeston of the Cockpit theater. Beeston lent him six pounds, for which Brome agreed to write a play.[16] Salisbury Court's management, disturbed by the possible defection of their playwright, then paid Brome ten pounds—after he turned over a new play—and promised to release Brome from his obligation to Beeston. But Salisbury Court again fell behind in payment, and Brome turned once more to Beeston. At this point Salisbury Court took the case to Sir Henry Herbert, Master of the Revels, who often settled such disputes. Herbert awarded Brome six shillings a week and five pounds for every new play he brought to the company. These amounts were to be paid by Salisbury Court until the plague abated enough for the theaters to reopen, which they did on 2 October 1637.

Brome's plays must have been highly profitable for Salisbury Court, because, despite continued arguments, they offered him a new contract in 1638. Orally, at least, he agreed. The new contract, this time a seven-year contract, called for Brome to write three plays a year as well as the plays he still owed Salisbury Court from the previous contract. He was to be paid twenty shillings a week plus a day's profit from each play. He was not to publish his plays without the company's consent. By 1639, however, he was again writing for Beeston. According to Brome, he had

14. Charles W. Wallace, who discovered the documents, briefly discusses them in "Shakspere and the Blackfriars," but he did not publish them or reveal their location. Ann Haaker rediscovered them and published transcriptions in "The Plague, the Theater, and the Poet."

15. Haaker, "The Plague, the Theater, and the Poet," 303. Italics within the quotation are Haaker's and indicate that, because the ink faded, she had to read the text from impressions in the paper.

16. Brome fulfilled this agreement with *The Antipodes*, 1636/37, which was first printed as a quarto by John Okes for Francis Constable in 1640.

been badly treated at Salisbury Court, he had never signed the second agreement, and he had gone with Beeston's company "as hee hopeth was and is law*full for* him so to doe."[17] Salisbury Court claimed to have been paying him; he denied it. In any case, Salisbury Court protested the loss of his services and filed the Bill of Complaint. The disposition of the case is unknown, but Brome continued to write for his friend Beeston.

Of his private life, we know little more than that he had a family; he mentioned his family's need in his response to Salisbury Court's complaint. Records of a child's christening and of several marriages include the name of Richard Brome, but these records are inconclusive: Brome was a common name, and no other sources confirm any of the records. As with many of his fellow dramatists, Brome's personality must be inferred from his writing and from a few contemporary comments about him. This is, of course, a highly subjective process. He seems to have been a moral man, a hard-working professional who took his writing seriously, and a plain-speaking man who disliked much of what he saw as court frivolity. His writings contain frequent mention of his humility. Maybe he *was* humble and hated to seem to have forgotten his beginnings, or maybe he found advantage in reminding audiences of his relationship with Jonson (which they were unlikely to forget in any case). Or it could be that he found that a pose of modesty allowed him freedom as a satirist.[18] His satire reflects more amusement with the world than disgust, although references to his poverty are frequent enough to explain more bitterness than he usually reveals.

The years after 1642, when the Puritans closed the theaters, must have been difficult for Brome. Despite the fact that he was deprived of his livelihood, he continued to work. He might have written "Juno in Arcadia," an entertainment, for the queen's arrival at Oxford in 1643.[19] If so, he was one of many literary men who sought refuge at Oxford during the Civil War. He wrote commendatory verses on Fletcher that appeared in the 1647 Beaumont and Fletcher Folio. In 1649, he edited *Lachrymae Musarum*, a collection of elegies written on the occasion of the death of Henry Huntingdon, Lord Hastings. And, in 1652, he dedicated the quarto of *A Jovial Crew* to Thomas Stanley; in that dedication, he described himself as "*poor and proud*" and said: "*You know, Sir, I am old, and cannot* cringe, *nor* Court *with the powder'd and ribbanded* Wits *of our daies: But, though I cannot* speak *so* much, *I can* think *as* well, *and as* honourably *as the best.*"[20]

17. Haaker, "The Plague, the Theater, and the Poet," 306.

18. Shaw, *Richard Brome*, 32.

19. John Cutts, "The Anonymous Masque-Like Entertainment in Egerton MS. 1994, and Richard Brome."

20. *The Dramatic Works of Richard Brome* 3:343, 344.

A year later, the man whom Thomas Dekker had called "*Son and Friend*,"[21] the familiar of Jonson, Heywood, Ford, and Fletcher, was dead. Alexander Brome (no relation), who edited two volumes of Brome's plays, prefaced the 1653 volume with mention of Brome's death:

> *for the Author bid me tell you, that, now he is dead, he is of* Falstaffs *minde, and cares not for* Honour.[22]

The English Moor is part of his legacy.[23]

Dates of Performance and Composition

In *Five New Playes* (1659), *The English Moor* is described as "A Comœdy as it was often acted with general applause, by Her Majesties Servants." Since the reorganized Queen Henrietta's Men began performing at Salisbury Court in 1637, and Brome was the playwright at that theater from 1635 to 1639, the play was undoubtedly first performed there sometime between 1637 and 1639.

The play is generally believed to have been the first one to be presented at Salisbury Court after the theaters reopened on 2 October 1637.[24] The prologue in the 1659 text alludes to the recent plague and mentions the players' hopes that they may not see such times again.[25] The prologue does not include specific references to the play, but since the play and the prologue were placed together in the 1659 text, they were most likely performed together at some time—if not at the first Salisbury Court performance, then probably during the next few weeks.

The hiatus because of the plague had been a long one—seventeen months with only a week's respite in February—so Brome would have had time to compose both *The English Moor* and *The Antipodes*, which was

21. Dekker, Commendatory verses to Brome's *Northern Lass*, in Brome, *Dramatic Works* 3:xi.

22. Alexander Brome, "To the Readers," in Richard Brome, *Dramatic Works* 1:iv.

23. Extant are fifteen plays plus one collaboration (see Bentley, *Jacobean and Caroline Stage* 3:55–92) and numerous commendatory verses. He has been suggested as co-author, with William Cavendish, of *Lady Alimony* (John Freehafer, "Perspective Scenery and the Caroline Playhouses," 111); as author of an entertainment, "Juno in Arcadia" (Cutts, "Anonymous Masque-Like Entertainment"); and as author of other prologues and revisions.

24. Frederick G. Fleay, *A Biographical Chronicle of the English Drama*, 39; Bentley, *Jacobean and Caroline Stage* 3:67–68.

25. This prologue could be the piece Brome referred to—in his response to the Salisbury Court Bill of Complaint—as "one Introduccon at theire first playing after the ceasing of the plague" (Haaker, "The Plague, the Theater, and the Poet," 305), although it is unclear what there is about this prologue that would distinguish it as an introduction.

likely the play he gave Beeston.[26] *The English Moor* could be the play Brome gave Salisbury Court once they agreed to pay him ten pounds; in any case, the play was probably written between May 1636 and October 1637.

The praeludium to T[homas?] G[offe?]'s *Careless Shepherdess*—almost certainly written by Brome for a Salisbury Court performance, which probably occurred in 1638[27]—contains a section that both strengthens the case for a 1637 Salisbury Court performance of *The English Moor* and connects an actor with a role. In the praeludium, Landlord, a country gentleman, and Thrift, a citizen, discuss what they find important in a play.

> *Landl.* Why I would have the Fool in every Act,
> Be't Comedy, or Tragedy, I 'ave laugh'd
> Untill I cry'd again, to see what Faces
> The Rogue will make: O it does me good
> To see him hold out's Chin, hang down his hands,
> And twirle his Bawble. There is nere a part
> About him but breaks jests. I heard a fellow
> Once on this Stage cry, *Doodle, Doodle, Dooe,*
> Beyond compare; I'de give the other shilling
> To see him act the Changling once again.
> *Thri.* And so would I, his part has all the wit,
> For none speaks Craps and Quibbles besides him:
> I'd rather see him leap, laugh, or cry,
> Then hear the gravest Speech in all the *Play.*
> I never saw *Rheade* peeping through the Curtain,
> But ravishing joy enter'd into my heart.[28]

26. Kaufmann also suggests that both plays were written during the plague closing (Kaufmann, *Richard Brome*, 63n).

27. G. C. Moore Smith suggests Brome as the author of the praeludium and the prologue (Smith, "The Canon of Randolph's Dramatic Works," 323); Bentley also believes that Brome might be the author and further proposes a date of 1638, since *The Antipodes*, which is mentioned in the prologue, was acted in 1638, and Brome was no longer with Salisbury Court in 1639 (*Jacobean and Caroline Stage* 4:503–4). I agree with a date of 1638 or early 1639 and am almost certain that Brome was the author. In his response to Salisbury Court's Bill of Complaint, he said he "hath made divers scenes in ould re*vive*d playes *for them* and many prologues and Epilogues" (Haaker, "The Plague, the Theater, and the Poet," 305). As Bentley noted, the praeludium contains disdainful references to plays written by nonprofessional city gentlemen and courtiers, and Brome, the professional, never hid his feelings about them (*Jacobean and Caroline Stage* 4:503). The author refers to wordplay, which Brome loved, as "out / of fashion" since the vogue of "sublime conceits." *The Antipodes* is directly mentioned in the prologue. Opportunity, tone, complaints, and play reference all point to Brome.

28. [Richard Brome?], "Praeludium for Thomas Goffe's *The Careless Shepherdess* (c. 1638)," 32.

Gerald Eades Bentley notes that this section of the praeludium seems to refer to Thomas Middleton and William Rowley's *Changeling*.[29] But since Brome is believed to have been the author of both the praeludium and the prologue and since the description fits *The English Moor*'s changeling, Buzzard, so closely—compare "*Doodle, Doodle, Dooe*" with Buzzard's oft-repeated "toodle loodle looe" (*TEM*, IV.iv)—Landlord and Thrift are more likely to be discussing *The English Moor* than *The Changeling*. "*Rheade*" is Timothy Reade, a popular comedian and dancer.[30] If he originally performed the role of Buzzard in 1637, he would indeed have acted "the Changling" on the Salisbury Court stage not long before the performance of *The Careless Shepherdess* there. Certainly it was to Brome's advantage to use the praeludium to remind audiences of one of his own plays.

Sources

The English Moor's basic plot lines—a child's revenge for a parent's murder, young lovers thwarted by an older generation, and attempts to cuckold an old man who has married a young wife—originated in antiquity and were so often adapted during the Renaissance that they are impossible to trace to an individual literary source; the analogues are too numerous. Nor does there seem to be a single, direct source for the particulars of the plot. In writing the play, Brome drew from several sources, especially the works of Jonson and Middleton.

His most pervasive debt is to Jonson. Scholars generally agree that Brome had Jonson's *Epicoene* (1609) in mind as he created *The English Moor*.[31] The comic plots are similar: an older, foolish man marries, is tricked by a disguise, demands a divorce, and is humiliated when the truth is revealed. If the debt were limited to the plot, it could only be said that Brome and Jonson wrote similar Plautine comedies. But Brome borrows further from Jonson's scenes, characters, and lines. Truewit's warning about the dangers of marrying a young woman (*E*, II.ii) parallels the gallants' warning to Quicksands (*TEM*, I.iii), and Sir Amorous La-Foole's comment about his ancestors (*E*, I.iv.37–68) parallels Buzzard's similarly silly remark (*TEM*, III.iii.66–67). The *charivaris* given to Morose and Quicksands are analogous. Truewit believes that his efforts

29. Bentley, *Jacobean and Caroline Stage* 2:540.

30. In *The Stage-Players Complaint*, Reade is mentioned as having "nimble feet," and the character representing him recalls having "capoured over the Stage as light as a Finches Feather" (254, 256). That Reade's name could be used in the title indicates his familiarity to Caroline audiences.

31. The relationship between the plays was first examined some time ago; see, for example, Andrews, *Richard Brome* (1913), 87–89, and Charles E. Guardia, "Richard Brome as a Follower of Ben Jonson" (1938), 31–32.

have saved his friend Dauphine (*E*, II.iv), just as Nat believes that his fun has worked to Theophilus's benefit (*TEM*, II.i). Morose and Quicksands are equally outraged at the supposed impudence of the women they've married; Morose's cries—"O, o, o" (*E*, III.vii.46, 49)—are also Quicksands's when he becomes convinced that he has been cuckolded (*TEM*, IV.iv.224). And both men discover the truth during "legal" proceedings in the final scenes. Morose calls the character Epicoene "a PEN THESILEA, a SEMIRAMIS" (*E*, III.iv.56–57)—the exact words Rafe uses to comment on Dionisia's valor (*TEM*, III.v.24).

Brome would have known Jonson's masques well. He may have been remembering Jonson's *Masque of Blackness* (1605) as he chose the Moorish disguise and composed the Moors' masque (*TEM*, IV.iv). When Brome wrote this masque, he certainly must have remembered Jonson's *Gipsies Metamorphosed*. In 1621, when *The Gipsies Metamorphosed* was first performed, Brome would have still been in Jonson's employ and was probably striving to become a dramatist. In Brome's scene, the Moorish actor's palmistry and even phraseology recall Jonson's Egyptian gypsies.

Brome was also strongly influenced by Middleton, although Middleton's influence is less obvious than that of Jonson. It has often been remarked that other Brome plays derived from Middleton's city comedies; the comic plot of *The English Moor* also has Middletonian characteristics. The action occurs in a world where, for many people, sex and money are intimately tied: Testy uses financial phraseology to describe the marriage he has forced on Millicent (*TEM*, I.iii.13–14); Quicksands sees her as "wealth" (*TEM*, III.i.27); Nat assumes that Theophilus's loss of Millicent is secondary to the loss of her portion (*TEM*, I.ii.94–95); Nat brags of his conquests and suggests, when he casts Phillis off, that she might turn to prostitution (*TEM*, I.ii.8–9); and—except for the play's final scene—Nat and the other gallants (who are as interchangeable as Tweedledum and Tweedledee) could have been transplanted directly from one of Middleton's city comedies. The changeling motif—that of a character who acts the idiot to accomplish another goal—links *The English Moor* to the comic subplot of Middleton and Rowley's popular tragedy *The Changeling*, even though the characters' motives differ. It would have been difficult to compose a changeling scene without thinking of this successful and often-revived tragedy; even the use of the word *changeling* would have evoked its memory.

Brome's revenge plot is also reminiscent of *The Changeling*. Brome opens the play with hints of unnatural tragedy; the audience sees, as Arthur does not, that Dionisia is a woman who intends violence. She is much like the character Beatrice in *The Changeling*. Dionisia is thoughtless, capable of quick changes, and driven by one obsession after another—it is as though she can only hold onto one thought at a time.

When she sees Theophilus (*TEM*, IV.ii), she falls in love as quickly as Beatrice does when she sees Alsemero, and thoughts of revenge must be banished while Dionisia concentrates on love. Even more significantly, when Dionisia and Rafe are together, the audience is reminded that "[s]uch braue spirited women / Haue cherishd strong-backd servingmen ere now" (*TEM*, II.iii. 20–21). Indeed, the audience is kept both intrigued and uneasy by the potential for a sexual relationship like that which exists between Beatrice and De Flores; the possibility is interesting, but if it were realized, the plot would take a far more serious turn. Even when Dionisia comically beats Rafe, an act that would seem to allay the fears of the audience, one recalls that Beatrice also scorned De Flores and that he, like Rafe, found encouragement there: "Women have chid themselves abed to men" (*TC*, II.i.88).

Dionisia and Beatrice are not completely alike; they couldn't be, since Brome planned a comedy, not a tragedy. Dionisia is wittier and more independent than Beatrice—a pseudovirago—and Brome mocks her while at the same time preparing the audience for her redemption. Whereas Beatrice says she wishes she had been made a man (*TC*, II.ii.107–8) but hires De Flores for the murder, Dionisia dons a pistol to do the killing herself—and falls in love instead. Despite these differences, the resemblances of characters and similarities in tone, particularly sexual overtones, make it seem probable that Brome was conscious of *The Changeling* as he wrote the revenge subplot of *The English Moor*.

It has been suggested that Brome drew from Shakerly Marmion's *Fine Companion* (1633): the "resemblance of the *English Moor* 1.3 to the *Fine Companion* 2.4 and 3.5 is quite apparent."[32] The situations are indeed similar. Littlegood, a usurer in *A Fine Companion*, attempts to persuade his daughter Aemilia to marry old Dotario, but—like Millicent in *The English Moor*—she puts off her would-be husband by threatening to make him a cuckold. In her father's presence, she seems to come to an agreement with Dotario, then—again like Millicent—escapes to marry the young man she loves. The most striking parallel is between Aemilia and Millicent, modest young women who become immodest in order to discomfit old men. But modesty pretending to be immodesty is sufficiently common in plays of this period, and the two characters are sufficiently different otherwise, that *A Fine Companion* might better be regarded as a significant analogue rather than as a source. Brome may have been thinking of *A Fine Companion* as he drafted Millicent's bawdy scene; if so, it is to his credit that he effected such a lively transformation.

32. Andrews, *Richard Brome*, 111; Joe Lee Davis also remarks on the similarity in *The Sons of Ben*, 192. Both Andrews and Davis mistake Testy's relationship to Millicent in calling him her father.

The Play

In *The English Moor*, Brome weaves together three plots, two of them city-comedy plots—which incorporate cynicism and worldly satire—and the third a romantic revenge plot—which involves noble ideals and splendid acts. Characters who normally inhabit different dramatic worlds, and for whom different standards of moral judgment apply, are placed side by side in this play, and each world view is found wanting. Brome undercuts the excesses of both city-comedy cynicism and romantic idealism by allowing the contrast between the two to serve as a corrective and by including in each plot characters who possess a genuine balance—they can combine sense, which the completely romantic characters lack, with sensibility, which the completely cynical characters scorn.

In the title plot, a city-comedy plot, Millicent, the young heroine, has been forced by her uncle, Testy, to marry Quicksands, an aging usurer. When the audience first sees her, Testy is bullying her to "love" Quicksands; he insists: "I'll see yo^{u} loue him presently. Soe, to bed" (*TEM*, I.iii.28). Both Testy and Quicksands confuse sex and love. They discuss the marriage consummation as though it were a business transaction, which, for them, it is. Luckily, Millicent sees that a part of her value as merchandise lies in her "Virgine blushes" (*TEM*, I.iii.38), and she reduces her worth by acting "cheap": she strokes Quicksands, sings snatches of bawdy songs, and plays on Testy's earlier demand by querying: "Will yo^{u} see Vncle / How I will loue him? Prithee come away" (*TEM*, I.iii.96–97). Her boldness has the desired effect. Quicksands turns from lechery—"My edge is taken off" (*TEM*, I.iii.98)—to a fear of being cuckolded, a fear that is immediately reinforced by the local gallants' mythological horn masque. Cuckoldry, they suggest with extravagant display, is the inevitable result of an enforced marriage.

Millicent's initial reaction to the horn masque is relief at Quicksands's continued discomfiture and her reprieve, but she's also aware that she has been insulted and that both camps think they have power over her honor. The next morning she calls an end to pretense with the speeches that define her character:

> My honor is mine owne; and I am noe more
> Yo^{r}s yet (on whome mine Vncle has bestowd me)
> Then all the worlds (the Ceremony off)
> And will remaine soe, free from them & yo^{u}
>
> . . . .
>
> Till yo^{u} recant yor willfull Ignorance,
> And they their petulant follies.
>
> . . . .

Both they & yo^{u} trench on my peace & honor,
Dearer then Beauty, Pleasure, Wealth & Fortune.
. . . .
If Honor fall (wch is the Soule of Life)
Tis like the damned, it nere lifts the head
Vp to the light agen. (*TEM*, II.ii.45–64)

She *is* an honorable woman, and a desperate one at this point in the play, since she has "worth" again (and bawdiness will not work twice). Her second ruse is a request to keep a one-month vow of chastity, because, she says ironically, she has been slighted by being denied the consummation of her wedding night.

Having heard Millicent speak about honor, Quicksands nonetheless disguises her in blackface, an act that underscores his inability to value her properly. He has heard the words but not understood the meaning, since genuine honor is not part of his world. He wants to feel safe and thinks that blackening Millicent will guard her virtue by making her unattractive to the gallants. He is, as Arthur says later, the "man that had but could not know her" (*TEM*, IV.iii.160). Ironically and appropriately, the disguise provides Millicent with the opportunity to rejoin her love, Theophilus; and it so inflames Nat that he commits the "deed of darknes" (*TEM*, IV.iv.190) with the disguised Phillis, thereby—much to the gallants' glee—convincing Quicksands that he has, as he feared, been made a cuckold.

The second plot, as common to London city comedies as is the humiliation of a usurer, concerns a gallant and his cast-off mistress, who seeks to marry him. In their first scene, Nat not only refuses to marry Phillis; he also suggests that she should be grateful to him: "I wish yo^{u} were more thanckfull m^{ris} *Phillis* / To one, has taught yo^{u} a trade that yo^{u} may liue on" (*TEM*, I.ii.8–9). Her response is to curse him. So far they fit their stereotypes. When Phillis next appears, she is a chambermaid to Lucy. Some of what she says indeed seems appropriate to the city-comedy servant; when the romantic Theophilus vows to live only by the memory of his lost Millicent, Phillis pragmatically replies:

Surely, good S^{r}, in my opinion
Sharpe eager stomachs may be better fed
Wth th'aiery smell of meat, then the bare thought
Of the most curious dainties. (*TEM*, II.i.128–31)

The contrast between the two is humorous, but as she undercuts his romantic posture, she also slightly sullies herself. The irony works both ways: Theophilus's excessive idealism highlights her lack of it as surely as her words emphasize his lack of realism. Although Phillis lives by her London-comedy wits throughout the play, Brome has given her sensibility as well. Lucy hires Phillis because of something that strikes her as genteel, and Phillis's pain is obvious when the discussion turns to false lovers. After Phillis learns of Lucy's secret love for Arthur, she is solicitous and encouraging; as the witty servant, she covers up for a distressed Lucy when Theophilus seems close to uncovering the cause of Lucy's pain. Later, Theophilus fires Phillis and she is hired by Quicksands; while in his employ, she has much the same relationship with Millicent: they are not equals, yet they are friends. It is only at this point that the audience learns that Phillis is of good birth and that six years earlier her father had been ruined in a lawsuit and had been forced to leave the country. Since then, she has been on her own, apparently working as a servant, at least part of the time for Nat. She supports Millicent's attempt for freedom with honor, but sadly fears that her own honor "is soe crackt / W^th^in the Ring, as 'twill be hardly solderd / By any art" (*TEM*, IV.iii.22–24). In assuming Millicent's disguise to help her escape, Phillis finds the means to make Nat her husband. Unlike many of her city-comedy counterparts, when she says she loves Nat "best of any liuing man" (*TEM*, IV.iv.198), she means it. She is not as noble as Millicent, but she is characterized by a balance of practicality and honest, virtuous emotion.

Throughout much of the play, Phillis's lover, Nat, seems the typical city-comedy gallant; in fact, he is the leader of the gallants. He makes it clear that he is not interested in love—just sex and mirth. He boasts of the number and variety of women he's seduced (*TEM*, III.iv.57–69); careless bawdy humor seems to be the note to know him by. He isn't evil—characters who sing and dance rarely are—he's just cynical. But Brome hints of something more—and with good reason, since Nat must be an appropriate mate for Phillis. Nat loves mirth more than seduction; Phillis's "innocent Mirth" (*TEM*, III.ii.3) should suit him ideally. More significantly, he misses her, although he acknowledges it only in a casual remark to Arthur; when Arthur suggests that Nat boasts about his women, but doesn't know which woman he really loves, Nat responds: "Not I (cadzookes) but all alike to me, / Since I put off my [Wench] I kept at Liuorie" (*TEM*, III.iv.55–56). Nat's initial response to his unsuspected betrothal to Phillis befits his stereotype—he is hardly gracious—but Brome has prepared us to accept Nat's reformation, which occurs when Nat assures Phillis that he'll be faithful: "I'll not mock thee. I bobd too much before" (*TEM*, V.iii.221). For Brome a "happy ending" means that Nat must renounce cynicism and embrace marital fidelity.

The third plot, a romantic one, concerns two pairs of siblings who are involved in both revenge and love. Before the play begins, Meanwell and Rashly, who have long been good friends, have supposedly argued and gone to France to settle their differences by duel. As the play opens, their children assume that both men are dead and—according to the romantic code—that those deaths dictate revenge. In the first scene,

Meanwell's daughter Dionisia urges her brother, Arthur, to take revenge against the Rashly family, Lucy and Theophilus: "[B]eare it out, til it proceed to Action" (*TEM*, I.i.28). Arthur does not want to take revenge; he tells Dionisia that the man who actually killed their father isn't in England and that Dionisia should "coole thy passion / Wth reasonable meanes" (*TEM*, I.i.40–41). What he doesn't say is that he loves Lucy Rashly. The audience, attuned to the conventions of romantic drama, may here sympathize with Dionisia as she cries: "Must I now play the Man, whilst yo^{u} inherit / Onely my Mothers puling disposition?" (*TEM*, I.i.49–50). The sex roles seem to have reversed: Arthur is the quiet, even-tempered one, and Dionisia is the forceful, passionate avenger.

When Dionisia discovers that her brother loves Lucy, she takes revenge into her own hands. She is reminiscent of *The Changeling*'s Beatrice, although she is more excessively romantic. Her noble rant is cut short, however, when she meets Theophilus and immediately falls in love with him, thereby committing the crime for which she so belittled her brother: loving an enemy. Her "unnatural" behavior—donning a man's clothing and attempting revenge—and its irrationality—she is avenging a murder that never occurred, as most members of a contemporary audience would have quickly understood—are punished in the play's last act. She is to be forgiven as part of the general reconciliation, but she is also chastised, and she is the only young central character who does not achieve her love. Instead she must repent the behavior that could have led to tragedy:

> S^{r} take noe thought for me
> Till my strict life,
> In expiation of my late transgression
> Gainst Mayden modestie, shall render me
> Some way deserving th'honor of a husband. (*TEM*, V.iii.203–7)

Arthur seems ingenuous at times. He is easily tricked by his sister, seeming to be "a model of guilelessness."[33] His response on first seeing Millicent as she flees Quicksands's house is that she must be a ghost—he even registers astonishment that the "ghost" speaks (*TEM*, IV.iii.214)—and the scene is both melodramatic and funny. Just as Phillis, a city-comedy character, becomes real by taking on romantic virtues, so Arthur, a romantic character, becomes real because he has sense. He is not weak—he fights valiantly for Theophilus, and he does so generously, fighting for the single man beset by many—but he stays out of the way of Theophilus's hasty temper and vengeance. He plans to reconcile the family divisions rather than kill because of them. He is the voice of reason at the Moor masque as he urges Quicksands against hasty vows and

33. Margaret A. K. Webb, "Richard Brome, Caroline Dramatist," 101.

convinces Testy of the injustice of the enforced marriage. When Millicent escapes, she chooses him as the best man to protect her. His reward for virtue and sense is a marriage to a fit mate—Lucy.

Rashly's son and daughter, Theophilus and Lucy, are Dionisia's and Arthur's counterparts, but within traditional sex roles. Theophilus is quick-tempered, eager for revenge, and capable of quick changes of mood; his humor, according to Arnold, is "to be deadly angry on / The least occasion; and be frends as quickly. / Hot & cold in a breath" (*TEM*, I.ii.162–64). His language and ideals are of the highest; he tells Arnold: "Twere greife & shame too, to an honest Manhood / To haue dishonor touch the thing he lou'd" (*TEM*, I.ii.177–78). He is not, however, sensible. When Nat tells him about the horn masque performed for Quicksands, Theophilus threatens to kill him, but only after he leaves the house, "For here it were inhospitable" (*TEM*, II.i.219). Through Dionisia and Theophilus, Brome pokes fun at romantic notions and, by implication, at the court of Queen Henrietta Maria, where interest in dramas of platonic love and the niceties of honor was eroding support for Brome's forte—vigorous humours comedy. But with Theophilus, Brome had a problem that he did not have with Dionisia: despite Theophilus's lack of sense, he has to be worthy of his love, Millicent. Brome solved the problem not by making Theophilus reasonable, but by making him, like his father's friend, "mean well." Theophilus's intentions are good, and he is generous and caring; it is just that his hasty humor gets in the way. As Arnold notes, Theophilus has "[t]he Noble nature still" (*TEM*, I.ii.216). Lucy is less active than many of the other characters, but she, like Arthur, is both noble and sensible. She is compassionate: she tries to ease Theophilus's pain over losing Millicent, and she tries to shield others from Theophilus's temper. She consistently urges reason and echoes Arthur's words to Dionisia when she says to Theophilus: "O brother y'are to passionate" (*TEM*, III.ii.39).

The fathers, Meanwell and Rashly, who provoked the revenge, appear in Act V, having returned to England. They had not gone to fight a duel, as they had told their children; their trip had instead been for the purpose of redeeming Phillis's father, Winlosse, whom they had undone in "a sad suit at Law" (*TEM*, V.i.66). Like Theophilus, they mean well and act rashly: their cause was good, but to pretend to have gone to duel was hasty and could have resulted in tragedy. They had assumed that their children would not try to avenge their deaths: "Where doe yo^u^ find / Sonnes that haue liues & Lands will venter both / For theyr dead Fathers" (*TEM*, V.i.30–32). The first audiences doubtless appreciated the social comment, but within the context of the play, the assumption is proved wrong. Together, Meanwell and Rashly are the deus ex machina of the plot, but in this play, the "gods" are not perfect.

The interweaving of the three plots makes for a complex play. Some critics have found this complexity disturbing. Even Swinburne, who generally praised the play, wrote: "[I]t might have been better than it is if both characters and incidents had been fewer."[34] To other critics, however, the play is an intellectual delight. R. W. Ingram, for example, notes that the plot "could stand as a display piece of Brome's ingenuity and control."[35] The shift in dramatic worlds within the play has been disturbing to some readers as well; historically the tendency has been to judge characters by the norms of either city comedy or romantic drama, but this is not possible in *The English Moor*. Brome has undercut both forms by shifting the value systems so that the contrast shows the excesses of each.[36] Indeed one of the play's major points is that neither extreme is the right way to look at the world.

There are a few minor plot inconsistencies; for example, if Meanwell and Rashly are neighbors, and Arthur and Lucy know each other well enough to be in love, surely Dionisia would know the Rashlys. This and other inconsistencies, I expect, would disappear in performance. Even the play's detractors have conceded that it is an excellent acting play.[37] Brome is, as a rule, "very hard served by relegation to the study: his liveliness and clever handling of character and movement, and of musical sound, need the appreciation best offered by live performance."[38] An audience would be involved with the production's visual humor and spectacle in a way that a reader would not be.

The English Moor is, in fact, a tour de force of showmanship. An audience would love Millicent's transformation from a put-upon innocent to a wanton woman who controls the situation—and the stage. Her "play" is immediately followed by the gallants' nine-character masque—a dumb show with commentary, violin and cornet music, dance, and costumes, including stag, ram, goat, and ox horns. In Act III Quicksands paints Millicent's skin onstage; the act also includes a tavern scene replete with local color and cries for the waiter and wine—indeed, Buzzard drinks so much of the wine that he has to be helped off the stage (a theatrical ploy that still works). The action pauses in Act IV while the page sings to Theophilus a song of mourning (which may or may not have been humorous—see the explanatory note to IV.ii.56). The stage becomes active enough, however, during Quicksands's Moorish masque, which

34. Swinburne, "Richard Brome," 505.

35. Ingram, "The Musical Art of Richard Brome's Comedies," 229.

36. On this point, see also Ellen Dutton Kiehl, "The Comedy of Richard Brome," 236–41.

37. Adolphus William Ward, for example, disliked the idea of painting the heroine but admitted: "[A]s an acting play this comedy deserves praise" (Ward, *A History of English Dramatic Literature to the Death of Queen Anne* 2:340).

38. Ingram, "Musical Art of Brome's Comedies," 240.

begins when Phillis, beautifully dressed as an exotic Egyptian princess and wearing splendid jewels, is escorted onto the stage by a Moorish actor. He proceeds to read the gallants' palms, after which the Moors dance to music. Nat then calls for an energetic galliard and dances "vily" with Phillis. The scene also includes Buzzard and Arnold's changeling act, in which Buzzard, as the idiot, spins with a rock and spindle and dances about the stage singing his "Toodle loodle looe."

One of Brome's outstanding qualities as a playwright is his ability to make his plays highly theatrical, and nowhere is this better illustrated than in *The English Moor*. The characters themselves "act" for a variety of reasons: Millicent to avoid consummation with Quicksands, Dionisia to test Arthur, Arthur to hide his love for Lucy when Dionisia feigns love for Theophilus, and Phillis to find employment with Quicksands. Previous to the play's action, Rashly and Meanwell created a false argument scene and spread the false idea that they were leaving the country to duel. Rashly refers openly to a shared sense of theatrical history when he says that he and Meanwell did not leave the country simply to test their sons as in the "old Play-plotts" (*TEM*, V.i.41). The three major set pieces in the play are not introduced for their spectacle alone, as a lesser playwright might have done; they are, rather, essential to the plot. The gallants' allegorical horn masque convinces Quicksands that the gallants are a threat, and it causes him to make plans for retaliation. He lets the gallants think they have won and then designs a masque in order to humiliate them in the same manner that they have humiliated him. His Moorish masque is based on the legend of a royal black woman who is destined to become white when she marries a white man. Millicent, of course, is to play the regal bride. Millicent's disguise allows Phillis to substitute for her. During the masque, the Moorish actor considers each of the gallants as a possible husband and rejects each for a reason that is embarrassing because it is accurate: "I plainely see / You haue sold & spent yor Liues Annuity" (*TEM*, IV.iv.47–48). Quicksands's retaliation proceeds as planned, but his triumph is short-lived; Buzzard and Arnold's changeling antic allows the gallants to regain the upper hand, and it soon appears that Quicksands has been cuckolded. In this scene, then, a masque counters a masque and is then countered by a changeling "play"; theatricality itself is a "tool of manipulation."[39]

As a satirist, Brome is gentle—more Horatian than Juvenalian. In *The English Moor*, he may mock both cynicism and romanticism, but he allows for a Shakespearean ending, in which everyone who has been mocked can change, can see right and wrong, and can understand the justice of

39. Jackson I. Cope, *The Theater and the Dream*, 142. On the masques, see also Ingram, "Musical Art of Brome's Comedies"; and Catherine Maud Shaw, "The Dramatic Function of the Masque in English Drama," 174–80.

it all. Even Quicksands "*yeild*[s] *to Fortune w*th *an humble knee*" (*TEM*, V.iii.224). Some people might find Brome's balance of reason, love, and justice the most romantic notion of all; in this sense *The English Moor* must have been comforting to spectators who were weary from the long months of plague and death.

Printed Texts

The play was entered in the Stationers' Register on 4 August 1640:

> Master Crooke. Entred for his Copies . . . six Playes vizt. . . . vjd. CHRISTIANETTA. The Jewish gentleman. A new Academy or Exchange. The love sick Court. The Covent Garden. and The English Moore or mock Marriage by Master. RICHARD: BROOME.[40]

In 1640, Brome was with Beeston at the Cockpit and apparently felt free to arrange for the publication of plays written under his Salisbury Court contract. *The Antipodes* and *The Sparagus Garden* were published that year. But *The English Moor* was not published until 1658–1659, so it may be that Salisbury Court was able to delay its publication, or perhaps the 1640 entry in the register was intended only to reserve copyright.[41]

The English Moor is the first play in the 1659 *Five New Playes*. (An earlier volume with the same title, which appeared in 1653, did not include *The English Moor*.) This volume was published by Andrew Crooke—an important publisher of plays and the man whose name was on the 1640 entry in the Stationers' Register—and Henry Brome, also a noted publisher of plays[42] (who is not believed to have been related to Richard). Two title pages exist for *The English Moor*: one that is dated 1658—on which the publishers' names are included, the author's name is omitted, and the Latin motto is incorrectly printed—and one dated 1659—on which the publishers' names are omitted, the author's name is included, and the Latin motto has been corrected.[43] Although the existence of the two title pages for the play suggests that the publishers might have intended to publish the play separately in 1658, this is not necessarily the case—the mistakes in the motto and the omission of the author's name

40. Edward Arber, ed., *A Transcript of the Registers of the Company of Stationers of London* 4:491.

41. Evelyn May Albright, *Dramatic Publication in England*, 236.

42. Henry R. Plomer, *A Dictionary of the Booksellers and Printers*, 56, 34.

43. The 1659 motto reads: "*Innocuos permitte jocos, cur ludere nobis Non liceat?*"—which can be loosely translated: "As long as innocent jokes are permitted, why should we not laugh?" In the 1658 motto, "Innocens" is mistakenly printed for "Innocuos," which garbles the Latin, and the comma is omitted.

would, in themselves, have been sufficient grounds for the printing of the cancel.[44] Among the extant copies of *Five New Playes, The English Moor* appears in three states: with both title pages, with the original title page only, and with the cancel only.

The exact nature of the copy used in the 1659 edition of *The English Moor* is not known, but one can speculate about it. The plays in the 1653 *Five New Playes* came from Brome's friend, Alexander Brome; in "To the Reader" in the 1659 volume, we are told that the stationers "bring these *Poems* as they had them from the *Author*"; and the 1659 *Five New Playes* includes commendatory verses by T. S. (generally believed to have been Thomas Stanley) that are entitled "To my most ingenious friend, Mr. *ALEX. BROME* Upon his setting forth *Mr.* RICH. BROMES *PLAYES*."[45] It is reasonable, then, to assume that a copy of *The English Moor* was given to the stationers by Alexander Brome, who had received it from Richard. The printed stage directions are full, and the song is missing, indicating that the copy was a playhouse book. (See "This Edition," below, for further description of the text.)

The 1659 text is an octavo and appears to have had a moderately careful printing; at least, few changes were made while the play was in press. The catchword "PROLOGUE" on A2^{v} is misplaced in all the copies I have seen, which suggests that after the forme had been made up, the prologue and the dramatis personae were transposed.[46] I have collated thirty-one copies of this edition, and only ten variants, mostly accidentals, were recorded, nine of them in Act I. (For complete lists of these variants and of the copies that I have collated, see "This Edition," below.)

The play next appeared in print in the second volume of *The Dramatic Works of Richard Brome Containing Fifteen Comedies Now First Collected in Three Volumes*, which was published in London by John Pearson in 1873. The composition was not particularly careful. In bibliographies, R. H. Shepherd is frequently cited as the editor, but his name does not appear in the volumes. This text was reprinted in New York by AMS Press in 1966.

The Manuscript

The manuscript of *The English Moor,* which Brome presented to his patron William Seymour, is located in Lichfield Cathedral Library, where it was deposited with the rest of Seymour's books in accordance with the

44. W. W. Greg, *A Bibliography of the English Printed Drama to the Restoration* 2:906, n. 1.
45. Brome, *Five New Playes*, sig. 1A7^{r}.
46. Greg, *Bibliography* 2:906, n. 2.

1673 will of his widow, Frances.[47] *The English Moor* is Lichfield MS. 68.

Despite the many references to it in bibliographies and critical studies, the manuscript has attracted little serious attention. In a list of books at Lichfield that was compiled in 1888, it was mistakenly noted as a quarto.[48] Early in this century, when Clarence Andrews contacted the Bishop of Stafford, the librarian at Lichfield, he was assured: "[T]here seems to be nothing of particular importance about the manuscript in the way of marginal notes, etc."[49]—which is true; but Andrews did not check to determine whether the text itself differed significantly from the published version, and he included only a few sentences about the manuscript in his book on Brome. In 1934, Bernard M. Wagner found that the dedication had not been printed, and he published its opening and closing lines.[50] Surprisingly, he ignored the also-unpublished prologue and song. Most other published references to the manuscript have been even less substantial than those I have just mentioned.

The dates of the manuscript's composition and presentation to Seymour are uncertain. The years 1636–1637—when the play was most likely written—and 1652—when Brome is believed to have died—are the outer limits. Some political references that were included in the octavo are missing from the manuscript, but this fact is not particularly significant; the references might have been written by another hand sometime before 1659, and even if Brome wrote the lines, he was too sensible to have included them in a copy intended for a man who held or had held high positions in the government of Charles I. A composition date in the late 1630s or early 1640s seems most probable. Brome's *Antipodes*, published in 1640, was also dedicated to Seymour, and the tone of that dedication, which begins: "The long experience, I have had of *your Honours* favourable intentions towards me,"[51] seems slightly warmer than that of *The English Moor*'s dedication—which suggests that *The English Moor* might have been presented in or before 1640; but tone is flimsy evidence on which to build a case. Brome would have most needed assistance from a patron when the theaters were shut down because of the plague in 1636, 1640 (when, in addition, he was involved in the Salisbury Court lawsuit), and 1641, and after the Puritans closed the theaters in 1642. Watermarks in the paper indicate that the manuscript may have been written in approximately 1640, since the paper is similar

47. The relevant provision reads, in part: "[A]nd for the respect which I and my family haue receiued from the City of Litchfeild I giue the Library and bookes which were my late deare husbands to the Church of Lichfeild to be putt in the new Library there" (London, PRO, Wills, Probate 355, fol. 133). Frances died in 1674, and the will was proved in 1677.

48. *Lichfield Cathedral Library: A Catalogue*, 119.

49. Andrews, *Richard Brome*, 37.

50. Wagner, "Manuscript Plays of the Seventeenth Century."

51. Brome, *Dramatic Works* 3:227.

to that used for a 1640 declaration by Charles I,[52] but I have not been able to determine when such marks first appeared, and it is impossible to ascertain how long the paper might have been lying about before it was used. It has been suggested that Brome is the author of "Juno in Arcadia," a masquelike entertainment that was probably performed at Oxford in 1643.[53] Though there is no other evidence of Brome's presence in Oxford then, the theory is an attractive one. There is no record of Brome during the early years of the Civil War; it may be that he was one of the men of letters who fled London and sought refuge with the court at Oxford. Plays were being performed there, and the manuscript paper is like the paper used at court. Also, Seymour was in Oxford in 1643: in November, he was among those who elected a new professor of astronomy;[54] and he was made chancellor of the university that year.[55] Unless more facts are uncovered, however, the dates of the manuscript's composition and presentation cannot be accurately gauged. The late 1630s or early 1640s remains the best estimate.

The manuscript is in excellent condition and is bound in limp, white, seventeenth-century vellum, measuring 290 by 190 mm. The vellum is gold-tooled, with the title of the play lettered in gold on a red leather rectangular label measuring 65 by 90 mm. The words "ECCL. CATH. LICHFIELD" appear with the title; therefore, either the manuscript was bound in its present form after it was received into the library's collection, or the label was added to the already-existing binding.

The manuscript contains seventeen sheets of paper that are folded in folio format. The first and last sheets contain library information and also form part of the binding, and the other fifteen sheets are devoted to the play. The second sheet has the title page on the second recto. The third sheet has the dedication on the first recto, the prologue on the second recto, and the list of characters on the second verso. Sheets four to sixteen contain the play proper; they were folded, written on, and lightly numbered from one to thirteen on the upper left-hand corner of each initial recto of a gathering. When the prefatory materials were added, the writer foliated the play in the upper right-hand corner of each recto, beginning with the title page as one; the following leaves are numbered consecutively through twenty-nine.

Two watermarks appear in the fifteen sheets of play materials. The first, which appears on the sheet containing the title page, is the image of a pot topped with a crescent moon. I could not locate a similar mark in Briquet or Churchill, but Churchill has suggested that such marks

52. W[illiam] A. Churchill, *Watermarks in Paper*, nos. 525, 527.
53. Cutts, "Anonymous Masque-Like Entertainment."
54. William Douglas Hamilton, ed., *Calendar of State Papers* 18:498.
55. *DNB*, s.v. William Seymour.

generally indicated French paper,[56] which was common in England in the mid-seventeenth century. The second watermark, which appears on all of the other sheets, shows two urns connected by an oval containing letters that appear to be "MV." The urns and surrounding figures are very close to Churchill's mark 525, while "MV" could be the "ML" of Churchill's mark 527 with a wire loosened. Churchill discovered marks 525 and 527 on paper in the aforementioned declaration issued by Charles I in 1640.

The dedication and the list of characters were written in a neat, set italic hand; the dedication is signed "Richard Brome" in the hand of the dedication, but a different ink appears to have been used for the signature. The prologue and the play text are in a mixed hand, that is, one in which secretary and italic graphs are mingled,[57] with the speakers' names and stage directions in italic.

The introductory material and the text were probably both written by one person. B. S. Benedikz, a Birmingham scholar who analyzed the manuscript in 1974, believes that this is the case,[58] and, based on my study of spelling habits and the handwriting, I concur. Brome may have transcribed the manuscript himself, but this is difficult to determine, since the only known sample of his handwriting is a signature on a 1632 deposition,[59] and signatures vary so greatly that they are not considered conclusive evidence in determinations of handwriting. The signature in the manuscript, however, corresponds with the handwriting in the rest of the manuscript, and, even if Brome employed a scribe, he probably would have signed the manuscript personally; the signature, then, points to Brome. Benedikz has stated that he feels that the handwriting in the manuscript is Brome's. In his 1974 assessment of the manuscript, he recorded "[o]ne hand (the author)"[60]; in a 1977 letter, he explained:

> Palaeographically the hand is of the right period; the codex is clearly a presentation copy to the noble patron . . . and it is exceedingly unlikely that Broome, any more than Sir William Kingsmill in another Somerset MS, would have employed an amanuensis on a copy destined for a recipient so important to him—certainly it would have been against all the code of behaviour of the time.[61]

56. C. M. Briquet, *Les Filigranes*; Churchill, *Watermarks*, 86.

57. Anthony G. Petti notes that the mixed hand was common at this time, "probably partly due to the fact that by this time both hands were employed with such frequency by any given writer that the graphs were interchanged almost involuntarily" (Petti, *English Literary Hands from Chaucer to Dryden*, 20).

58. Benedikz, *Lichfield Cathedral Library: An Interim Catalogue*, 33.

59. London, PRO Req. 2/732. The deposition and manuscript signatures are not identical, but could well have been written by the same hand. I was alerted to the signature by Ann Haaker, Letter to James L. Harner, 24 July 1978.

60. Benedikz, *Lichfield Cathedral Library: An Interim Catalogue*, 33.

61. Benedikz, Letter to S. J. Steen, 24 October 1977.

Scribes were occasionally employed to write presentation copies—Suckling hired a scribe for the copy of *Aglaura* that he presented in 1637 to Charles I—but it was unusual, and Brome was not a wealthy man. Even Jonson wrote the presentation copy of his *Masque of Queenes*.

An examination of the writer's handling of verse and prose suggests that Brome is not the writer of the manuscript, but this evidence is inconclusive. The tavern scene (*TEM*, III.iii) and the antic scene (*TEM*, IV.iv) contain parts that could be expected to appear as prose; in the octavo, the speeches of III.iii do appear in this form. But in the manuscript, the capitalization and the line divisions in the speeches of III.iii and IV.iv vary, sometimes appearing as prose and other times as verse. If it is assumed that a dramatist would automatically have written such speeches as prose, it might therefore be concluded that the writer was not a playwright. But it could be that Brome either was not concentrating on the copying or, like many writers then and now, was not concerned about the niceties of form. And since the mixture of styles that appears in the manuscript also appears in the octavo version of IV.iv, format cannot become a deciding factor.

The writer often continued writing past a line-ending and then—realizing that he should have started a new line—crossed out letters or words. (See, for example, the manuscript notes to I.i.30 and II.i.270.) This could have occurred because the writer was familiar with the text—as Brome obviously was—but by itself this is not strong evidence, since a scribe could just as easily have read beyond a line-ending and failed to start a new line. But on another occasion, the writer, instead of following the text, began to use a phrase that had been employed elsewhere in a similar context. (See the manuscript note to II.iii.64.) Once the writer continued a line beyond a line-ending and then omitted the line he'd begun; an otherwise fairly careful scribe probably would not have done this, but an author would have been able to do it without qualm. (See the manuscript note to V.iii.204.) The combination of these instances suggests that the writer knew the text.

And finally, in the dedication Brome states:

> *on confidence of both, I*
> *am enbouldned to offer, this Issve of some*
> *leasurable howers to the Iustice of your mercy.*

Brome was not one of the fashionable gentlemen who lightly referred to their plays as lines dashed off in a few hours; he was a professional dramatist—writing was his livelihood. In his response to Salisbury Court's 1640 Bill of Complaint, he testified that he had initially been unwilling to agree to the contract, knowing that three plays a year was "more then hee *could well performe*."[62] Brome, then, would not likely have referred to one of his plays as an "*Issve of some / leasurable howers*"; the copy, however, could reasonably have been thought of as such a product, and Brome would have had hours of leisure during the plague closings and after 1642. This evidence does not prove that the hand was Brome's, but it does indicate the probability.

This Edition

> Brome deserves to be more read than he is, and first of all to be more accessible than he is.
>
> T. S. Eliot[63]

The text for this edition is from Brome's presentation copy of the manuscript. Even though most of the text of the octavo printed in 1659 is probably Brome's work, its transmission is uncertain and therefore so is the origin of the variations. Alexander Brome might have obtained his copy of the play from Richard, but there are indications within the text that it was written as a playhouse book, and, to a dramatic company, an author's manuscript generally was "simply another theatrical commodity, like a cloth cloak or laced cuffs"[64]—prompters, actors, and other playwrights freely made revisions. Had the play been in repertory for some time—the 1659 title page states it was "often acted"—the revisions might have been extensive. Therefore, even if the text used in the octavo was at one time in Richard's possession, we cannot be sure of its course after leaving his hands—whether it was with the company, or when it was obtained—so we cannot ascertain which of the possible alterations, deletions, or additions were written or approved by Brome. The manuscript, on the other hand, is a clean text in a single hand—probably the author's—that Brome at some time found acceptable as a presentation copy.

The manuscript text is significant because it differs greatly from the printed text and is therefore an addition to the Brome canon; moreover, with the publication of this text, the scholar can study a Brome play in two complete forms, each of which appears to be a "good" text rather than a bad quarto re-created from an actor's memory. Although the possibility exists of a revising hand or hands in the octavo, the likelihood is that the play as it appears in that version is mostly Brome's; therefore a

62. Haaker, "The Plague, the Theater, and the Poet," 301.
63. Eliot, "Imperfect Critics," 21.
64. Gerald Eades Bentley, *The Profession of Dramatist in Shakespeare's Time*, 87.

comparison between the texts can further understanding of the play, of the changes Brome (or someone else) made in the play, and of the differences between a presentation text and a theater text.

The two texts are virtually the same length, but, as the collation shows, they vary a great deal in other respects. Because Brome could expect that his presentation copy would be read rather than be used as a performance text, he included his formal song in its proper position instead of putting it on a separate sheet, as he would have done with a company copy. As a result, we have the lyrics to "*Loue*, where is now thy Deitie" (*TEM*, IV.ii.39–55), a song that adds substantially to our knowledge of Brome's use of lyric. The manuscript also contains a different prologue, in which Brome mentions what detractors had said about his work but does not refer, as the octavo prologue does, to the idea that his company had recently had trouble with the authorities; perhaps Brome thought it safer not to mention a political problem to a court official like William Seymour. In any case, Brome offers Seymour a different prologue, one that provides more evidence of the resentment he felt toward those who criticized him for not writing the more up-to-date romantic dramas of "lofty language" and subject.

Some of the variations between the texts can be attributed to the fact that the manuscript was intended for Seymour. Political references in the octavo have, in some cases, not been included in the manuscript. For instance, in the octavo, Nat notes that being called before the High Commission (of which Seymour was a member in 1641, and with which he had been associated earlier) would be worse than cutting one's throat or swallowing poison (see "Collation," I.ii.47). It is understandable that Brome did not include such lines in the presentation copy. The octavo epilogue, in which Brome links "*to fly from truth*" with "*and run the State*," is also not included in the manuscript. If Brome wrote the presentation copy after the beginning of the Civil War, satire that would have been effective when he composed the play would, by that time, have lost much of its humor anyway. The octavo contains a few more references to London than the manuscript does—such as Quicksands's comment about the black actor having made speeches before "my Lord Marquess of *Fleet* Conduit" (see "Collation," IV.iv.20); some of these references might have been political allusions, but they no longer seem relevant because the referent has been lost. Whether such political comments and allusions to London were comic additions to the stage version or were deleted from the presentation copy is impossible to determine; given Brome's care to omit what could be wrongly (or rightly) interpreted as derogatory, the latter is at least as likely as the former.

Other differences exist because the 1659 text was a theater copy. In that version, as noted above, the song is omitted, since songs were not included in the books prompters used. Although the stage directions in both texts are complete, with entrances and exits clearly marked, the octavo's descriptions of the action are more specific. For example, when the drunken Buzzard is led off stage in III.iii, the octavo even notes the song—"Down, *Plumpton-parke*"—that the actor is to sing.

Other variations, not attributable simply to the distinction between presentation and theater copies, concern larger issues of structure and characterization. The most significant structural differences occur in Act III. In the first scene of both texts, Quicksands paints Millicent to keep her "safe" and hires Phillis. From that point on, however, the sequence of the action varies between the two copies. In the manuscript, the next scene follows directly from what has just occurred; it picks up with Lucy's distress over Phillis's dismissal, moves to Arnold's announcement that Millicent has run away, and concludes with Arnold's dismissal and Theophilus's hatred of Quicksands. Scene iii is the tavern scene, in which the gallants plan their changeling antic; and in Scene iv Nat runs into Arnold, who has just been dismissed, and engages him to complete their group. Structurally, then, Act III in the manuscript text opens with Quicksands's plan to outwit the gallants, follows with the results of those actions on Theophilus, moves to the gallants' new plan to humiliate Quicksands, and ends with the addition of Arnold to the group; the act breaks into two parts: plot and counterplot. In the octavo, however, the tavern revelations immediately follow Quicksands's painting of Millicent; then the scene with Lucy, Theophilus, and Arnold occurs; and finally Arnold encounters Nat (this time with Edmond and Vincent onstage). The placement of the tavern scene before the Lucy/Theophilus scene results in a shifting back and forth in the act—from plot to counterplot, then to the results of the first plot, and back to a continuation of the second plot. The order of the manuscript emphasizes the Quicksands/Theophilus conflict, since the two are juxtaposed, while the octavo's sequence sharpens the audience's sense that the conflict is between Quicksands and the gallants. In the octavo, the conflict between Quicksands and Theophilus is further diminished by the omission of Theophilus's imprecations and his vow of vengeance. Perhaps the scenes were transposed in the acting version merely to allow for a smoother transition, in which Arnold, after being dismissed, remains onstage, reacts to his plight, and is immediately joined by the gallants; however, the order of the scenes does make a difference in our understanding of the central characters and the action.

The character Quicksands is fundamentally the same in both versions, but the focuses of the two texts are somewhat different—in the manuscript text, he speaks slightly less than in the octavo, and other people speak about him slightly more. In III.ii of the presentation copy, Theophilus, as noted before, verbally attacks Quicksands, calling him a villain, and vows vengeance. In IV.iii, Phillis and Millicent discuss Quicksands's propositioning of Phillis, thus preparing the audience for Millicent's accusations against her husband in Act V and, at the same time, altering the viewers' perceptions of the women's motivations. Edmond and Vincent open V.iii with brief comments about Quicksands and his tight-fisted usury. None of these speeches occurs in the octavo. But the octavo does contain a longer speech by Quicksands than the manuscript does—in which he exults in his victory over the gallants, recites all the taunts the "cozen'd people" have thrown at him, and laughs at "their foul errors" (see "Collation," IV.i.21). This section might have been added when another of Quicksands's speeches from this scene—the comparison of Millicent's natural beauty and her "Ebon Casket" (*TEM*, IV.i.6–11)—was shifted to, and expanded in, the painting scene in Act III (see "Collation," III.i.89). The characterization of Quicksands is good in both versions of the speech, but in the painting scene it also serves to prolong the tension of the scene and to give the actor words that suit the action as he covers Millicent's face with black paint.

In the manuscript text, Dionisia seems a little more violent and a little less the noble woman whose redemption seems appropriate. In III.v Rafe comments:

> Soe many of these tryalls [beatings] haue past vpon me
> That all my flesh is beaten into brawne.
> And my head codled.

He likes it: "Her blowes kindle desire in me. They are my ticklings." But her aside to the audience at that point is confusing: "If I had not this fellow to beat sometimes / My fury would dye in me." How are we to interpret a character who maintains her "righteous" fury by beating a servant? The line is probably meant to exonerate Dionisia by indicating that without Rafe she would return to a more normal state, but it makes her transition to obedient daughter a little more difficult to accept. A later aside of Rafe's has a similar effect; when Meanwell tells Dionisia to resume feminine dress, Rafe says: "Now will shee beat me euen to death in priuate" (*TEM*, V.ii.155). These speeches are missing from the octavo.

Both texts maintain the sexual tension between Rafe and Dionisia, but it seems slightly greater in the octavo: Dionisia sets Rafe to spy on Arthur and promises to love him "everlastingly" for it (see "Collation," I.i.112); Rafe suggests that "[t]he warm touch of my flesh / Already works in her" (see "Collation," II.iii.66–68); Dionisia responds to one of Rafe's innuendoes with "I dare not understand thee yet" (see "Collation," III.v.27); and there is less emphasis on the beatings.

Other distinctions between the texts, although minor, are nonetheless instructive. Frequently words are shifted, separate words are contracted, or phrases are altered—a "thee" in one text is "you" in the other, and "gainst *Arthure* then" in one is "then against *Arthur*" in the other—for no apparent semantic reason. When the octavo was printed, a compositor could have introduced some variants as he read a couple of lines and then set what he remembered, changing the original somewhat; or perhaps he was short of letters or running out of space and so altered a word or made a contraction. But otherwise the octavo seems to have had at least a moderately careful printing, and it is unlikely that the compositor made so many changes—he would have been trying, after all, to set what was in front of him. It is also possible that the writer of the presentation copy changed the text while recopying it, especially if the writer was Brome himself. For example, in V.iii it seems that the writer chose to omit a line that appeared in his copy text (see the manuscript note to V.iii.204). But as was the case with the printing of the octavo, care was taken in the writing of the manuscript to be sure that incorrect words were deleted and correct words inserted. Considering the large number of minor variants (as well as the major variants discussed above), it is probable that both texts were taken from separate copies that differed slightly from each other. This could be because Brome—unless he was writing poetry—was more concerned with major characters and stage action than with the precise phrasing of a line. Edmond's and Vincent's names seem to have been used interchangeably; a line said by one in the manuscript is often said by the other in the octavo. Since the two characters are not really distinguishable from each other—they are merely "the gallants"—the reversals probably also reflect Brome's disinterest in details—in this case, in which gallant says which line.

The manuscript text sometimes makes sense of lines that were obviously misread by the compositor and of speeches that were partially omitted from the octavo. For example, the octavo's

Tes. For you must know
She is no Neece of mine that could transgress
In that *leane* kind

reads "In that *lewd* kind" in the manuscript (*TEM*, V.iii.82; italics mine in both quotes). And Nat's protestation, in the octavo, that he will marry the Moor

Or else, before you all, let me be torn
To pieces; having first those dearest members
In which I have most delighted, daub'd with honey

takes on a new meaning with the addition, in the manuscript, of the line "To be lickd off by the beares" (*TEM*, V.iii.77).

At least once, seemingly inconsequential variations force a new look at an entire passage. The manuscript text makes clear that the Host in V.i is meant to be a humorous fellow, in both senses of the word; his temperamental "humor" is to speak in rhymed verse. After several lines of the Host's bad verse, Rashly comments: "Thou keepst thy humor still my riming host"; and the Host completes the couplet: "My humor was, nor is, nor must be lost" (*TEM*, V.i.25–26). Later, however, he switches out of rhyme to speak more seriously: "And wthout Rime I'll tell yo^{u}" (*TEM*, V.i.68). The compositor of the octavo misread two words and replaced "riming" with "running" and "Rime" with "ruine"; thus, the point is lost.

The play in the manuscript is not a better play in all ways than *The English Moor* we have read before—some of the lines that occur only in the 1659 text are genuinely effective—but it is better in some ways and deserves to be made more generally available.

The manuscript has been transcribed at least once before, by W. G. Hergest in 1928 for an unpublished University of London master's thesis. His handwritten transcription, a typescript, and a carbon of the typescript, each bound individually, are in the Lichfield Cathedral Library. A great deal of research on seventeenth-century graphs has been done in the interim, and the accidentals and the substantives in Hergest's transcription are often inaccurate. For example, the last line of the prologue in his typescript invites the audience to "grave" rather than "grace" the play and the players again. Once my transcription was complete, I compared it with his typescript and noted all variants between the two transcriptions; but since his typescript is inaccurate and has no authority, I have not included the variants here. The version of *The English Moor* that appeared in the 1873 collection of Brome's works and in its 1966 reprint (see "Printed Texts") obviously has no textual authority. While the octavo does not have primary authority, it is the only text (other than the presentation manuscript) that has any connection with Brome and that is, therefore, a relevant form of the text.

Accordingly I have located and collated the following thirty-one copies of *The English Moor* in the 1659 *Five New Playes*. The fourteen copies that are preceded by an asterisk were collated from xerox or microfilm, and the other seventeen were collated by physical examination:

BL–1 British Library; London; 162.C.21
BL–2 British Library; London; G18536
BL–3 British Library; London; E.1782
*CCFB Francis Bacon Library; Claremont, California
*CLU–C William Andrews Clark Memorial Library, UCLA; Los Angeles, California
*CSmH Huntington Library; San Marino, California

*CtY Yale University Library; New Haven, Connecticut
DFo–1 Folger Shakespeare Library; Washington, D.C.; Paine bookplate
DFo–2 Folger Shakespeare Library; Washington, D.C.
DLC Library of Congress; Washington, D.C.
*E National Library of Scotland; Edinburgh
*ICN Newberry Library; Chicago, Illinois
*ICU Joseph Regenstein Library, University of Chicago; Chicago, Illinois
*LL–B Brotherton Library, University of Leeds; Leeds
LVA–1 Victoria and Albert Museum; London; D25.E.44
LVA–2 Victoria and Albert Museum; London; D25.E.45
LVA–3 Victoria and Albert Museum; London; FD.15.7
MB Boston Public Library; Boston, Massachusetts
*MH Houghton Library, Harvard University; Cambridge, Massachusetts
MWiW–C Chapin Library, Williams College; Williamstown, Massachusetts
*MWiW–S Sawyer Library, Williams College; Williamstown, Massachusetts
*NcU Louis Round Wilson Library, University of North Carolina; Chapel Hill, North Carolina
*NIC Cornell University Library; Ithaca, New York
*NjP Princeton University Library; Princeton, New Jersey
*NN New York Public Library; New York, New York
O–1 Bodleian Library; Oxford; 8° B.14 Art BS
O–2 Bodleian Library; Oxford; Douce B. 334
OU Ohio State University Library; Columbus, Ohio
O–W Worcester College Library; Oxford
PPEF Edwin Forrest Home for Retired Actors; Philadelphia, Pennsylvania
PU Charles Patterson Van Pelt Library, University of Pennsylvania; Philadelphia, Pennsylvania

The OU copy was used as a control text, and only ten variants were recorded. (A "+" indicates that the variant occurs in a line that is not in the manuscript; it occurs in lines following the line number given.)

Sheet A (inner forme)

Uncorrected: DFo–2.
Corrected: BL–1, BL–2, BL–3, CCFB, CLU–C, CSmH, CtY, DFo–1, DLC, E, ICN, ICU, LL–B, LVA–1, LVA–2, LVA–3, MB, MH, MWiW–C, MWiW–S, NcU, NIC, NjP, NN, O–1, O–2, OU, O–W, PPEF, PU.

Sig. A5v
I.ii.42 Who, the] Who the
I.ii.43 prithe.] prithe
I.ii.53 married? quickly] married, quickly

Sheet A (outer forme)

Uncorrected: DFo–2.
First State Corrected: ICN, LL–B.
Sig. A6v
I.ii.133 Theoph.] Theo.
Second State Corrected: E.
Sig. A3r
I.i.9+ me I must. I must.] me I must.
Third State Corrected: BL–1, BL–2, BL–3, CCFB, CLU–C, CSmH, CtY, DFo–1, DLC, ICU, LVA–1, LVA–2, LVA–3, MB, MH, MWiW–C, MWiW–S, NcU, NIC, NjP, NN, O–1, O–2, OU, O–W, PPEF, PU.
Sig. A3r
I.i.9+ me. I must.] me I must. I must.
Sig. A4v
I.i.105 here, by] here by
I.i.112+ Do, and] Do and

Sheet B (outer forme)

Uncorrected: BL–2, CCFB, CLU–C, CSmH, CtY, DFo–1, DFo–2, DLC, E, ICU, LL–B, LVA–1, LVA–2, LVA–3, MH, MWiW–C, MWiW–S, NcU, NIC, NjP, NN, O–1, O–2, OU, O–W, PPEF, PU.
Corrected: BL–1, BL–3, ICN, MB.
Sig. B1r
I.iii.75 *Quic.* Is] *Quic* Is

Sheet F (outer forme)

Uncorrected: BL–1, BL–2, BL–3, CLU–C, CtY, DFo–2, DLC, E, ICU, LVA–2, LVA–3, MB, MWiW–C, MWiW–S, NIC, NjP, NN, O–1, O–2, OU, O–W, PPEF.
Corrected: CCFB, CSmH, DFo–1, ICN, LL–B, LVA–1, MH, NcU, PU.
Sig. F3r
(catchword) Hoping] Hopin

THE ENGLISH MOORE OR THE MOCK-MARIAGE

THE ENGLISH MOORE OR THE MOCK-MARIAGE

[1r]

To the thrice honorable [2r]
William, Lord Seamor
Earle of Hertford
Lord Beauchampe &c

My singuler good Lord

your noble disposition, your countenance to the freedome of comendable endeuours doe not more add glory to your owne Greatnes then encouragement to my weaknes in particuler. Your Candor and your Iudgment haue neuer vsed to conster a duty a presumption; on confidence of both, I am enbouldned to offer, this Issve of some leasurable howers to the Iustice of your mercy. This English Moore (my good Lord) is but an vnperfect coppie, the originall it self being the heart of the Presentor. Meane presents from men of low fortunes to personages of your inclination, finde sooner an entertainement of Charity then contempt; by which favor, the neglected Muses gather roome to breath in. In this tender of my service, to the constancy of your noble nature I am an humble

1–4. William Seymour (1588–1660), "by nature and habit a scholar," Earl of Hertford, Lord Beauchamp; Marquis of Hertford (1640) and Duke of Somerset (1660); Lord Chancellor of Oxford (1643–1647, and again in 1660); member of the Privy Council (1640); governor to the Prince of Wales (*DNB*). Dedicatee of Brome's *Antipodes* (1640).

5. *singuler*] excellent; often used when addressing persons of title.

10. *conster*] construe; i.e., you have never interpreted what is only my duty to you to be presumption.

17. *inclination*] nature, character.

petitioner, that your Lordship according to your wonted vertue will please to preserue in your good opinion, amongst the faithfullest of your seruants

Your Lordships,

Humblest

Richard Brome

Prologue [3r]

I come to welcome yee; and not to boast
o[r] Authors skill, our paines, or any Cost
in o[r] new play. Alasse wee dare not swell
aboue the hope youl finde it faire and well,
In gentle and ingenious acceptation.
Tis faire and free from anie personation;
Noe Lady greate or lesse, or any Lord
States man or knight our humble Scenes afford.
All sorts may see't, and not them selues abusd
by Satyre or by Fawne: for none are v'sd
as persons heere, by whome it Cann bee said
this part by him, or her, was meant, or made.
It is noe flattering peece; nor ist a quarrell
against the tymes, men, manners, or apparrell.
And, for a truth is in't, as well at Rome
the Scene might haue been laid, as heere at home.
Tis nought then some doe whisper. I'st not so?
and that the poet has for gott his old wont. Noe?
then Ile goe further: heeres noe mirth, noe sport,
or very little, (thanck some body fort

6. ingenious] showing discernment.

7–13. Dramatists often alluded to or represented living persons; but spectators sometimes went overboard in their search for parallels and even brought notebooks with them in which to jot down the latest tidbits of gossip (William A. Armstrong, "The Audience of the Elizabethan Private Theatres," 248). Seymour probably would have approved of Brome's disclaimer.

11. Fawne] wheedling courtesy.

that said hee could write nothing else) what now
(the Subiect of the Play too being so low
that lofty language, or the purer glosse
of Poesie laid vpont, were extreame losse)
can you expect? I dare not prophesie:
but give vs leaue to hope (though all this bee)
You may finde some thing in't that may invite
you to grace it, and vs, another night

The Persons in the Play [3v]

Meanewell / *Rashly*	*Old Gentlemen*
Testie	*A Iustice of Peace*
Quicksands	*An Vsurer*
Arthure	*Sonne to Meanewell*
Theophilus	*Sonne to Rashlie*
Nathaniell / *Vincent* / *Edmond*	*young Gentlemen*
Arnold	*An old Serving man to Rashly*
Buzzard	*Seruant to Quicksands*
A Page	*to Theophilus*
Winlosse	*An antient Gentleman*
Rafe	*Seruing man to Arthure*
	Actors in the habit of Blackmoores
	An Host
Dionisia	*Daughter to Meanewell*
Lucy	*Daughter to Rashly*
Millicent	*Neece to Testy*
Phillis	*Daughter to Winlosse*
Madge	*Maidseruant to Quicksands*

23. too] *interlined with a caret MS.*

25. losse] i.e., a waste of "lofty language" and poetry.

Act i. Scene. i. [4^{r}]

Arthure. Dionisia.

Ar. Deare Sister, beare wth me.
Dio. I may not Brother.
What! Suffer yo^{u} to pine & peake away,
In yor vnnaturall melancholly fitts?
W^{ch} haue allready turnd your purer blood
Into a Toad-poole dye? I am asham'd
(Allmost, vpon my life) to call yo^{u} Brother
Ar. O my Sister—
Dio. I can say, ô my brother too; to shew yo^{u}
How it becomes yo^{u}; and haue the same cause
Equally wth yo^{r}selfe, to spend my life
In solitary mourning; and would doe it;
Could it make good o^{r} losse. My honord Father!
A teare has scap'd me there. But that's by th' by
And more of Anger gainst his Enemy;
And his foreuer curst Posteritie
That robd vs of a father, then of Sorrow
For what we know is vnrecouerable.
But to sitt grieuing oře his memory
In a resolued silence as yo^{u} doe;
Killing yor owne blood, whilst a veyne holds any
Proceeding from the flesh, that drew out his
Is meerly idle. Mingle then yor griefe
Wth thought of braue Reuenge: And doe it not
In priuate meditation in yor Chamber
But beare it out, till it proceed to Action.
Ar. By powring blood on blood.
Dio. By quenching fire
Of high Reuenge, wth base vnnaturall blood;
By stopping of our Fathers curelesse wounds,

30. fire] fire of ("of" *deleted*) *MS*.

8. Toad-poole dye] A toad-pool is a mass of corrupt, poisonous matter; therefore, with "dye," the phrase suggests a poisonous liquid the color of putrefaction—probably black, as melancholy was called the black distemper.

16. by th' by] incidental.

22. resolued] steadfast.

28. beare it out] i.e., keep the thought of revenge actively alive.

(W^{ch} still bleed fresh in o^{r} vext Memories)
Wth the prowd flesh of him that butcherd his.
Ar. We know he liues not, that has slayne o^{r} Father:
Or, if he liues, 'tis where I can not reach him.
He nere saw English herbour, since his sword
Vnfortunately had the better of my Father.
Dio. But his sonne liues.
Ar. Good Sister, coole thy passion.
Wth reasonable meanes.
Dio. If yo^{u} or I
Could wth o^{r} Sighes, or teares, blow hence, or wash
Away the memory of a Father; then
I could sit downe by yo^{u}, & end a life
As yo^{u} allmost haue done in Pensiuenes
By giuing way to Sorrow. Where's the Spirit
Which my slayne Father had? Haue yo^{u} noe ꝑt on't?
Must I now play the Man, whilst yo^{u} inherit
Onely my Mothers puling disposition?
Ar. I know thy drift (good Sister *Dionisia*)
Is not vnto Reuenge, or blood; but to
Put motion in me, to prevent the Daunger
A sad Retirednes might bring vpon mee.
Dio. Be it as yo^{u} thinck it, soe yo^{u} will abroad
And make the house noe longer darck wth Sighing. *Ent: Rafe*
Now S^{r}! The newes wth yo^{u}?
Ra: Newes worth the hearing.
Onely to laugh at; good for nothing ells. [4^{v}]
Dio. Is the old Ruffian tane, & hang'd, that causd
Our sorrow in my Fathers death? Or is
His finicall sonne braine-batterd; or his daughter
Become a prostituted publique shame
Ar. How merciles are yor wishes Sister!
Ra. Lady noe.
But as I was hanckring at an Ordinary,
In quest of a new Master (for this, here

48. ꝑt on't] part of it.
62. finicall] overly-scrupulous and precise.
62. braine-batterd] beaten about the head; gone mad. Cf. Brome, *The Queens Exchange*, III.i.21: "[H]e's brain-crack'd, lunatick and Frantick."
66. hanckring] hanging about, or loitering.

Will neuer last me to a new liuory,
'Lesse he were merrier) I heard the brauest noyse
Of laughter at a wicked Accident
Of Mariage, that was chopt vp this Morning—
Dio. What mariage? Quickly.
Ra: Who doe yo^{u} thinck has maried
Faire m^{ris} *Millicent.*
Ar: Is shee maried?
Theophilus (I can name him, though his Father
Was fatall vnto mine) was sure to her they say'd.
Ra: Yes, but wthout a Priest. She has slipt his hold,
And is made fast enough vnto another:
For wch fine Master *ThEO* soe whines & chafes,
And hangs the head. And there is sport for yo^{u} now.
Dio. It dos me good to heare of any crosse
That may torment theyr Family. I wish
Ioy to the Man that did beguile him of her
What ere he be.
Ar. But who has maried her?
Ra. Thence springs the Iest. Old m^{r} *Quicksands* S^{r},
The bottomles devourer of young Gentlemen;
He that has liu'd till threeskore od a Batchelor
By threeskore i'the hundred. He that has
Vndone by mortgages, & Vnderbuyings,
Soe many Gentlemen that they all despair'd
Of meanes to be reueng'd—
Ar. But where's yor Iest?
Ra. The Iest is, that now they haue found that meanes
(As they suppose) by making of him Cuckold.
They are laying their heads togither in euery Corner
Contriuing of his Hornes; and drincking healthes
To the Successe. And there were sport for yo^{u} now,

69. brauest] most excellent, abundant.
70. Accident] unexpected event.
71. chopt vp] done with unusual haste.
78. wthout a Priest] i.e., the marriage had not been solemnized.
87. S^{r}] sir; used in direct address to Arthur.
90. threeskore i'the hundred] an exorbitant rate of usury. Ten on the hundred is often mentioned as the legal rate of usury, though cases of twenty percent were not unknown. See R. H. Tawney's introduction to his edition of Thomas Wilson, *A Discourse upon Usury*, 37–48.
91. Vnderbuyings] the purchase of articles at a cost below their value because of another's need to sell quickly.

If yo^{u} were any body.
Ar. I'll abroad howeuer.
Dio. That's nobly sayd. Take Courage wth yo^{u} Brother.
Ar. And, yet, me thincks I know not how to looke
The wide world in the face, thus, on the sodaine.
Ra. For that S^{r} (looke yo^{u}) I haue here, by chance,
A Players beard, I borrowd wth a purpose
To haue put some Iest vpon you in yor sadnes.
Ar. Dos it doe well wth mee?
Ra. You'll neuer haue
One of yor owne soe good
Yo^{u} looke like *Hector* in it
Ar. Goe, Fetch my sword & follow mee— *Ex^{t}. R*
Dio. Why, now yo^{u} are my Brother.
Ar. Expect me towards th'euenning. Farewell, Sister— *Ex^{t}*
Dio. I hope he has some stratagem afoot
In o^{r} Reuenge to make his honor good
It is not Griefe can quit a Fathers blood.— *Ex^{t}.*

Scene. ii. Enter Nathaniel. & Phillis.

Nat. Pray thee be answerd; and hang off o'mee.
I'll ha'noe more to say to thee: Noe: Not I,
I meane i'th'way yo^{u} wot on, as I am honest.
Phil. I seeke not to yo^{u} the way yo^{u} wot on, I; [5^{r}]

114. Farewell,] *interlined with a caret MS.*

108. Arthur has put on the beard that he wears as a disguise through much of the play.

111. *Hector*] the valiant Homeric hero. To call someone a Hector was not always to compliment him, however. In N. B.'s *Court and Country; or, A Briefe Discourse betweene the Courtier and Country-man* (1618), Country-man defines city Hectors as those who "durst prate, lye, sweare and for sweare, scoffe and swagger, drinke and dice, drab and stab . . . and this was their valour" (in *Inedited Tracts*, 194). The Hectors of *The Hectors, or The False Challenge* (1656) are described by Alfred Harbage as "usual tavern blades" (Harbage, *Cavalier Drama*, 82).

Scene ii

2. hang off o'mee] let go of me (literally); stop bothering me (figuratively).

4. wot on] "Wot," in a general sense, means "know," as in "I wot it is true"; here, a more accurate paraphrase might be "are thinking of."

4. as I am honest] a phrase adding intensity; "as I am a gentleman" also was commonly used. In Phillis's response, she uses "honest" more literally than Nat means it.

But to require yo^{u} to be honest, & marry me.
Yo^{u} haue done too much the tother way allready.
Nat. I wish yo^{u} were more thanckfull m^{ris} *Phillis*
To one, has taught yo^{u} a trade, that yo^{u} may liue on.
Y'are not the first, by twenty, I haue taught it
That thriue well i'the world
Phil. There are soe many
Such Trade-teachers in the world; and soe few
Reformers, that the world is growne soe full
Of female Frailties, that the Harlotries
Can scarse allready liue by one another;
And yet yo^{u} would haue me thrust in among'em.
Nat. I doe not vrge yo^{u}. Take what course yo^{u} please
But looke not after me I charge yo^{u}. I
Am not markd out for Matrimony, 'thanck my stars.
Phil. Should I run euill courses yo^{u} are the cause;
And may in time curse yor owne act in it.
You'll find th'vndoing of an honest Mayd
Yo^{r} heauiest Sinne vpon yor bed of Sicknes.
Twill cost yor Soule the deepest groane it fetches.
And in that hope I leaue yo^{u}. *Ex^{t}.*
Nat. Farewell Wagtayle.
Marry thee quoth a! That's wise worke indeed.
If we should marry euery wench we touch
Twere after Six a weeke wth some of vs:
(Marry Loue forbid) when two is enough to hang one. *Ent Vincent*
Vin. *Nat*! We haue sought yo^{u} diligently, for feare *& Edmond.*

6. yo^{u}] *interlined with a caret MS.*

9. trade] i.e., prostitution.

15. Frailties] weaknesses; fallen women. According to the *OED*, the latter meaning is a modern usage; apparently the *OED* compilers did not note early examples of this usage, such as in *The English Moor.*

16. liue by one another] live because of one another; i.e., earn enough money because there are so many.

20. 'thanck my stars] In astrology, one's stars are the planets that, by their position at a person's birth, influence his or her temperament and destiny; here, used lightly.

23. Mayd] maiden; maid-servant. See II.i.65 and III.iv.56.

27. Wagtayle] colloquial expression for a wanton woman.

28. Marry thee quoth a] "Quoth a" means "said he" or "said she" and was used when repeating another's words with contempt or sarcasm; therefore this phrase is similar to the more modern "Marry thee, indeed!"

31. Marry] an oath, sworn by the Virgin Mary; here, a pun.

31. two is enough to hang one] i.e., for bigamy.

The newes that is abroad should fly before vs.
Nat. What newes? What flying fame doe yo^{u} labour wth?
Ed. Newes, that makes all the Gallants 'bout the Towne
Fly out o'their litle Witts: They are soe eager
Vpon the Ioy. I meane such as o^{r}selfes
That haue or sold, or mortgag'd; or bene cheated
By the graue Patron of Arch-Cosonage,
Whose sad misfortune we are come to sing.
Shall I need to name him to thee?
Nat. Who, the old Rascall *Quicksands*? Speake good *Vince.*
What has he hangd himselfe? Speake quickly pray thee.
Vin. Worse, worse by halfe man. Darst thou heare a newes
Whose mirth will hazard cracking of a Rib.
Nat. I, and't be two. Here's hoopes enough besides
To keepe my drinck in.
Vin. He'has married a young wife
Nat Has he Cadzookes
Ed. We bring noe comfort, wee!
Nat. Nere goe fine sport. What is shee, ha! What is shee?
'Would he had had my *Philly* was here eene now
What is shee? quick, what is shee?
Vin. One much too good for him. The beauteous *Millicent,*
Driuen by the tempest of her Vncle's will,
Is, like a Pinnace forc'd against the Rock.
Nat. Hee'll neuer split her, that's the best on't.
I hope shee'll breake his heart first. I'll be sworne
I thanck yo^{u} for yor newes; and know what I
Will presently goe doe.

34. flying fame] quickly-spreading rumor or report. "Flying Fame" was a ballad, which was possibly set to the music now associated with "Chevy Chase" (Claude M. Simpson, *The British Broadside Ballad*, 96–98).

34. labour wth] carry; work to bring forth, as in childbirth.

38. or sold] perhaps "o'ersold."

39. Patron of Arch-Cosonage] practitioner of great fraud and deception.

46. hoopes] ribs.

47. In *O*, several speeches are inserted here (see "Collation"). These speeches may have been added at another time, or they may have been omitted from the presentation copy because Brome feared to risk offense to a patron who was so highly placed in the government—Seymour was a member of the Privy Council and, thus, of the Court of High Commission in 1641 (G. E. Aylmer, *The King's Servants*, 11).

51. Nere goe] cant expression of indeterminate meaning. See also line 70.

56. Pinnace] small sailing vessel; woman, especially a mistress or a prostitute.

57. split her] break up the vessel; have intercourse with her.

Ed Pray stay alitle
And take vs wth yo^{u} S^{r}. What will yo^{u} doe?
Nat. That, wch we cannot doe all at once. Doe not hold me
Vinc. We came to cast a plot w'ye.
Nat. Cast a pudding
How long ha'they bene married.
Vin. But this morning. [5^{v}]
Ed. And therefore heare vs.
Nat. You'll ha'me come too late.
Nere goe tis shame, he was not Cuckolded
'Fore dinner.
Vin. That had bene a fine first course,
At a wedding feast indeed. Alitle patience
Nat. Pray let me take my course for Supper yet
Vin. Thou art not mad! Dost thinck shee's such a beast?
The busines longs to vs as much as yo^{u}.
He has wrongd vs all alike. He has cossend vs
As much as yo^{u}.
Nat. He has made mee soe poore
That my poore whore eene now had hope to had me.
Vin. The case is ours: His wrongs are common to vs;
Soe shall his wife be, can we purchace her.
To wch we must take time for best advantage;
And then o^{r} lotts, and turnes, & equall shares.
Did we bring yo^{u} the newes for yo^{u} to runne
And spoyle all p^{r}sently?
Nat. Pardon my Zeale good Gentlemen, wch onely
Considerd but the fitnes of the act;

63. That . . . once] i.e., make Quicksands a cuckold.

65. Cast a pudding] stuff meat and herbs into an animal intestine; or, roll pudding tobacco (Skeat); a punning response.

72. course] part of a meal; act of sexual intercourse. Cf. Brome, *A Mad Couple Well Match'd*, IV.iv.49–51: "[I]f you will not obey me in a course of further pleasure to night, fetch me a hundred peeces to take a course abroad."

75. not mad] used ironically.

76. longs] belongs.

82. purchace] obtain.

84. lotts] drawings to determine the order of rotation.

84. turnes] rotation, with a pun on acts of sexual intercourse. Cf. Shakespeare, *Cymbeline*, II.iv.142: "[N]ever count the turns."

84. shares] participation, with a possible pun on "pubic region, groin" (*OED*).

And that tis more then time 'twere done in sooth. *Ent.*
Ed. And see here comes a fourth man, that hast lost *Theophilus.*
More on her part then we vpon the Bridegroomes.
Vin. Hee's very sower, & sad.
Nat. Tis crept vpon him
By this vntoward accident. Twould anger
Any man to be nos'd of such a Match.
But I'll remoue his sorrow.
Ed. To him pray thee.
Nat. Gentle *Theophilus* yo^{u} are well met.
Yo^{r} sorrow is familier wth vs,
In the large losse of yor betrothed loue:
W^{ch} losse (I grant) may be a greater griefe to yo^{u}
Then that of yor deare Father: For, to speake
Plaine truth, the losse of fathers are good findings,
As this Age gouernes.
But S^{r} be comforted: yo^{u} haue o^{r} pitty
And o^{r} Reuenge to ease yo^{u}. Tis decreed
Her Husband shall be instantly a Cuckold.
Theo. Most sinfully thou liest; and all that giue
Breath to that foule opinion. *(Draw & fight.*
Nat. What doe yo^{u} meane?
The. Giue me that thought from thee: Nay from yee all
Or I will rippe yor hearts out.
Ed. Hold.
Vin. Forbeare
The. I'll haue that thought out first
Nat. I say he dos deserve to be a Cuckold.
Let him be what he will. A pox vpon him.

89–90. SD *Ent. / Theophilus.*] *Ent. Theophilus. / & Arnold.* ("*& Arnold*" *deleted*) *MS*; *Enter* The- / ophilus & / Arnold. *O.* 91. on] vpon ("vp" *deleted*) *MS.*

90–91. that . . . Bridegroomes] i.e., Theophilus has lost her marriage portion, which would have been more money than the gallants have lost to Quicksands.

94. vntoward] unfortunate.

95. nos'd of such a Match] beaten out of such a wealthy marriage.

100. betrothed] If the betrothal had been an *in verbis de futuro* contract—one spoken in the future tense as "I will" or "I shall"—then intent was expressed, but the contract did not bind either party unless consummation had occurred. Had the contract been *in verbis de praesenti*, or spoken in the present tense as "I do," then the contract would have been binding, with or without consummation (Carroll Camden, *The Elizabethan Woman*, 86–90). The latter contract, without consummation, seems most appropriate to the characters and the situation.

103. good findings] good events, as the sons inherit the estates.

Ed. Soe we say all.
The. What's that to ill in her?
I stand vpon that point. Man's euill merrit is
Noe warrant for a Wiues dishonestie.
I say had shee a Man forty degrees
Beneath her Vndeservings, it were more possible
For him to deceaue her wth a good life,
Then shee him wth a wicked.
Nat. I say soe too.
But then I say againe the more's the pitty.
The Doe & vndoe *(Fight againe*
Nat. Zookes, now yor bitch as bit me
I say he will be one; he shall be one;
I'll make him one my selfe *Ent: Arthure in his false beard: he fights on Theophilus part.*
Vin.Ed. And wee'll both helpe him.
Arth. This is oppression; an vnmanly one [6^r^]
Soe many vpon one! *Ent: Arnold.*
Arn. Why here's trim busines. Help, hoe Murder, Murder.
Nat. What devill's this is raisd?
Fall back: Twill proue a scirvy busines els. *Ex^t^. Nat: Vinc: Ed.*
Arn. Haue yo^u^ noe hurt S^r^
The. Noe I am confident.
Arn. By yor fauour I will see. *(He searches Theoph:*
Arth. I haue fought against my frends
(What Fortune's this) to saue mine Enemy.
But I hope neither know me. I desire
To rest hid to my frends for my offence;
And to mine Enemy, till I make him dearer. *Ex^t^.*
The. I told thee there was none.
Arn. I am glad it proues soe.

133. SD *part.*] *part. / Ent A Ent Arnold.* ("*Ent A*" *deleted*) *MS*. Since Arnold's entrance is also indicated at line 135, which appears to be the correct point of entrance, I have omitted it here.

122–23. had . . . Vndeservings] i.e., had she a husband whose faults were forty degrees worse than her own. "His" (i.e., Quicksands's) is substituted for "her" in *O*.

129. bitch as bit me] sword has hit me.

136. trim] excellent, used ironically.

137. devill's this is raisd] devil raised from Hell; the reference is to Arthur's valor and skill with the sword.

138. scirvy] scurvy, sorry or ill.

140. confident] certain, sure.

The. But where's the Gentleman?
Arn. Doe yo^{u} not know him S^{r}?
The. Not I. Tis the first time that ere I saw him.
And yet he fought for me.
Beshrew thy idler care that made me loose him.
What should he be, that soe could fight for me
Yet care not for my company? Beshrew thy heart
For searching me. Why should he vse me thus?
I am made beholding now to I know not whome.
And I am the worst to sue or seeke to a Man—
Arn. That scirvy betweene prowd & bashfull quallity
Yo^{u} are famous for, as tother toy that haunts yo^{u}
The. What's that?
Arn. Why, to be deadly angry on
The least occasion; and be frends as quickly.
Hot & cold in a breath. Yo^{u} are angry now
Wth him that fought for yo^{u} I warrant yo^{u}.
The. In truth I am; and frends wth them I fought wth.
He vsd me peeuishly to leaue me soe,
Ere I could thanck him.
Arn. Soe. Tis that I told yo^{u}.
The. But did yo^{u} marke the humanity of my Gentlemen?
'Cause shee's disposd by her old Vncles Will
On that Vnworthy *Quicksands* (deuill take him).
They thought twould sound like Musique in my eares
To heare her disgrace sung: When her faire honor
Is all I haue to loue now shee's tooke from mee;
And that they would goe about to rob me of.
Twere greife & shame too, to an honest Manhood
To haue dishonor touch the thing he lou'd.
Heauen grant me patience. O my slaughterd Father!
I am thy Sonne, & knowne by thy infirmity.
Arn. Me thincks S^{r} his example should allay yo^{u}.
Impatience was his ruine

181. Me] Me ("e" *written over* "y") *MS.*

167. peeuishly] perversely.

170. humanity] consideration.

The. Pish we see, Theeues dayly hangd for robberies yet some
Goe on still in the practise. What a Fine
Is set vpon the head of foule Adultery,
And yet o^{r} Neighbo^{r}s Wiues can hardly scape vs;
There's Law against Extortion, & sad penalties
Set vpon Bribes,
Yet great mens hands haue theyr Forefathers itch.
Nothing can banish Nature, thats the Morrall.
Arn. It was indeed yor Fathers knowne Infirmity.
But of yor Father, is there yet noe hope
Of better newes?
The. Noe: certainly hee's slaine.
Arn. I haue not heard a story of more wonder:
That two such men, of such estate & yeares
Having liu'd allwayes frends, & neighbo^{r}s nearly
Should, at the last, fall out soe mortally [6^{v}]
On a poore cast at Bowles. Where wast they fought?
The. It is vncertaine. All we heard of'hem
Was, they rode forth (Tis now a whole yeare past)
Singly to end their quarrell: But to what
Part of the kingdome, or the world they tooke
We can by noe inquiry find; or heare
Of either of them. Sure they crost the Seas;
And both are slayne.
Arn. Yo^{u} speake poore comfort S^{r}.
The. I speake as my heart finds. Shee's gone foreuer too.
Her hearts desire be wth her.
Arn. Now hee's there againe
The. Then my poore Sisters Sicknes, that torments me;
Neuer in health since o^{r} deare Father left vs.
Arn. And now there againe.

183. Pish] an exclamation; in accordance with his humor, Theophilus is immediately impatient.

184–85. What . . . Adultery] Adultery and the begetting of illegitimate children were crimes for which suspected offenders could be tried and, if found guilty, fined or whipped. See Maurice Ashley, *Life in Stuart England*, 24, 29.

189. itch] the itch of the palm, or greed.

199. cast at Bowles] In lawn bowling, a small ball, or jack, is cast (thrown) across the green; and the bowlers, in teams, then try to cast weighted balls—which run on the bias—as near as possible to the jack. (These speeches are quick exposition; Arnold was Rashly's servant, and he would have known what had happened and when.)

202. Singly] to engage in single combat, to duel.

The. How shall I doe to find these Men againe?
I shall not be at rest till I be frends wth them.
Arn. The noble nature still. twill shew it selfe.
The. I'll seeke'hem out. *Nathaniell* allwayes lou'd me: *Ex^{t}*
Arn. Here's an vnsetled humor. In these fitts
Hee'll nere be mad, nor euer well in's witts. *Ex^{t}.*

Scene. iii. Enter Testy. Quicksands. Millicent.

Tes. Goe to, I say, goe to. As y'are my Neece,
And hope t'inherit any thing, thats mine,
Shake off this Mayden peeuishnes. Doe yo^{u} whimper
Vpon yor wedding day? Or doe yo^{u} thinck
Yo^{u} are not married yet? Did yo^{u} not say
I *Millicent* take *Mandevill*? a ha!
Was it not soe? Did not I giue yo^{u} too?
I that haue bred yo^{u} from the Cradle vp
To a fit growth to match wth his faire yeares,
And far more faire estate?
Mil. I there's the Match.
Tes. And doe yo^{u} now beginne to cast yor Reckoning
As if I had not sommd it right? Goe to
Loue him I chardge yo^{u}.
Mil. I will indeauour't S^{r}.
Tes. Yo^{u} will indeauor't! Ist noe further yet?
Stand from her Nephue. I'll soe swinge her. ha?
Quic. Let me intreat yor patience. Shee's my wife S^{r}.
Tes. Dandle her in her humor; doe; & spoile her then
Quic. Tis but her Modestie.
Tes. Her sullen doggednes
I'll bast it out of her. Yo^{u} doe not know her, Nephue
Quic. I shall S^{r} before morning, I not doubt
Tes. Yo^{u} will indeauour't. Come I'll see it done.

23. Yo^{u}] Doe Yo^{u} ("Doe" *deleted*) *MS*.

13. cast yor Reckoning] literally, calculate your accounts; Testy, who has married his niece to Quicksands's fortune, uses financial terminology to query: "Are you now questioning my judgment?"

18. swinge] beat.

20. Dandle] pamper.

23. bast] beat soundly.

Marry a Man first, and then indeauour
To loue him; will yo^{u}? ha! Is it but soe?
I'll see yo^{u} loue him presently. Soe, to bed
Mil. What before supper
Tes. A Posset & to bed
Quic. Good Vncle be not yo^{u} soe rough & stiffe wth her.
I know my supple, tender dealing will
Get more vpon her Loue, then all yor Chidings
Tes. Such tender dealers spoile young brides; & get
Nothing but stubbornes. Downe wth her I say
Now in her wedding sheets: She will be naught else.
Mil. Construe more charitably, I beseech yo^{u},
My Virgine blushes.
Quic. Did not I tell yo^{u}, twas her bashfullnes? [7^{r}]
Tes. Would yo^{u} haue brided it soe lumpishly,
Wth yor spruce Younker, that fine silken Begger
Whose land lyes in yor husbands counting house
Or the most part?
Mil. O my *Theophilus*.
Tes. Would yo^{u} haue whin'd & pul'd had yo^{u} had him,
To bedward thinck yo^{u}? Yet (to speake the truth)
I neuer saw her laugh, nor heard her sing
In all my life: yet she could both I haue heard
In company shee lik'd
Mil. It has bene 'mong Maydens then.
But honord S^{r} (I know what I will doe)
To let yo^{u} see & heare, since yo^{u} desire
To haue me shew a Chearefullnes vnto
My reuerend husband, looke yo^{u} S^{r} I'll kisse him
Clappe him & stroke him; hang about his neck

35. her] *interlined with a caret MS.*

30. Posset] a drink composed of wine and hot milk, with sweeteners and spices sometimes added.

31. stiffe] cold and inflexible.

32. supple] accommodating.

34. get] also in the sense of "beget."

36. naught] nothing; also sexually promiscuous, wicked.

40. brided it soe lumpishly] acted the bride so dejectedly.

41. spruce Younker] dapper young gentleman.

41. silken] elegant in person and speech.

51. (I know what I will doe)] an aside.

55. Clappe him] pat him fondly or clasp him.

Ah my *Ioe* ah ha ha.
Quic. Hay day. Shee'll make me blush wer't possible
Mil. I'll sing him songs too.
Quic. Whoop! How's this?
Mil. Indeed I will Chick; Song as old
As thine owne selfe my Chick-a-bird
Quic. Chick did shee call mee? That's a common word
Wth wiues that cuckold their old cravend husbands
Mil. *Shee made him a bed of the Thistle downe soft,*
Shee layd herselfe vnder to beare him aloft: Sings
And euer shee sung, Sweet turne thee to mee,
Wee'll make the new bed cry Iiggy Ioggie.
Tes. What impudence is this?
Quic. Shee's gone as farre
Beyond it now, as it was to it.
Mil. Now may yo^{u} answere
Goe to bed sweetheart I'll come to thee Sings
Make the bed fine & soft I'll ligge wth thee
ha ha ha—
Quic. Is this yor bashfull Neece
Tes. What canst thou meane by this? Dos this become thee?
Mil. Pray doe not beat me o' my wedding day: But tell me
How this & halfe a dozen chopping children
Will sute an old mans wife some fiue yeares hence
Quic. O intollerable!
Tes. Ist possible thou canst doe this?
Mil. Let women Iudge. Tis very possible
That a young lusty wife may haue six children
By one at once in fiue yeares S^{r}. and by
One father too. I'll make him young enough
To father mine.

56. *Ioe*] a term of mock endearment. Cf. "He can say my Jo and think it not" (Tilley, M1343).

56. Innocence feigning wantonness was a fairly common theatrical device. Compare Millicent's ruse with that of Florimel in Fletcher's *Maid in the Mill* (1623).

57. Hay day] an exclamation of wonder.

60–61. Chick; Chick-a-bird] Words referring to chickens or birds are commonly applied affectionately to children; they are derisive and connote weakness when applied to a man.

63. cravend] weak or cowardly.

64. The snatches of song set down in this scene are often mentioned by later writers or in listings of songs of the period, but I have not been able to locate complete versions or definite sources.

73. *ligge*] lie.

78. chopping] strong and vigorous.

84. one at once] one at a time.

Quic. Shee'll make a Youth of mee.
Tes. Shee's mad; and I am amaz'd.
Quic. I know not what I am.
Mil. *There was a Lady lou'd a Swine: Honey quoth shee*
And wilt thou be true Loue mine. Hugfh quoth hee. Sings
Tes. Dee heare me Gentlewoman? Are yo^{u} in yor witts?
Mil. Yes, & mine owne house I hope. I pray be ciuill.
Shall wee to bed S^{r}, supperles? you need
Noe stirring meats, it seemes; I'm glad on't.
Come Biddy. come away. Will yo^{u} see Vncle
How I will loue him? Prithee come away.
Quic. My edge is taken off. This Impudence
Has mortified my Concupiscence.
And dasht me out of Countenance. What a beast [7^{v}]
Was I to marry? Rather what a beast
Am I to be, if a preventing witt
Be not in speedy readines?* O horrible!
A noyse of Sowgelders hornes wthin.
What hideous noyse is this?
Tes. Some mischeiuous plot I feare vpon o^{r} house.
Ent: Buzzard.
Buz. I cannot helpe it.
Whilst I went forth for the halfe pint of Sack
To make yor prodigall posset; and the Mayd,
(Watching the Milke for running ouer), forgot
To shut the dore, they all rusht in.
Tes. What are they?
Buz. Vizarded people S^{r}; and odly shap'd:
You'll see anon. They are tuning of their pipes;
And sweare they'll giue yee a Willyee Nill-yee daunce
Before yo^{u} goe to bed, though yo^{u} stole yor Mariage

90–91. This song snatch is especially insulting, since the hog was the accepted emblem for usurers. The frontispiece to John Blaxton's *English Usurer* depicts a hog, from whose mouth comes a balloon with the words: "Mine is the *usurers* desire, To roote in earth, wallow in mire." The usurer in Robert Tailor's *Hog Hath Lost His Pearl* (1614) is named Hog. On the association of usurers with swine, see Celeste T. Wright, "The Usurer's Sin in Elizabethan Literature," 193; and Arthur B. Stonex, "The Usurer in Elizabethan Drama," 196, 201. See also Tilley, M1005.

95. stirring meats] stimulating meats, or sweetmeats.

96. Biddy] chicken, fowl; term of derision.

98. edge] sexual desire, especially erection (Partridge).

104. *Sowgelders hornes*] the horns blown by those who gelded or spayed sows, to announce their arrival; swine were associated with usurers (see note for I.iii.90–91).

113. shap'd] costumed.

115. Willyee Nill-yee daunce] willy-nilly dance; i.e., a dance that will take place whether it is wanted or not.

Quic. Outragious Roysters.
Tes. Call out & rayse the street.
Mil. That were to let in violence indeed.
These are some merry harmeles frends I warrant.
I knew I could not be soe ill belou'd
Among the Batchelo^{r}s, but some would find
Way, to congratulate our honord Mariage
Quic. What wth horne-Musique?
Tes. A new kind of florish.
Well: Let'hem in. If they wrong vs to night,
The Law, hereafter, shall afford vs right.
Pray let's resolue to see't. Here comes their Prologue. *Enter Mercury.*

Merc. At a late Parliament, held by the Gods,
Cupid & *Hymen* fell at bitter ods,
Vpon an Argument, wherein each did try
T'advance his owne, 'boue tothers Deity,
Out of this Question, *W^{ch} might happier proue,*
Loue wthout Mariage, or Mariage wthout Loue?
By the effects the triall must be made;
Soe each from others office drew his ayd:
Cupid noe more of *Hymens* matches fram'd;
Nor *Hymen* married those, that Loue inflam'd.
Now marke the sad effects this strife begott
Cupid his fiery darts & Arrowes shot
As thick as ere he did; and equall hearts
Hee wounds wth equall Loue. But *Hymen* parts
Theyr forward hands (alasse) and ioyneth none,
But those, wch his new Match-maker brings on:
(Old greedy *Auarice*) who, by his spells,
In brests of Parents, & of Guardians dwells,
That force their tenderlings to loathed beds.
W^{ch} vncouth Pollicie to Sorrow leads
Thousands a thousand wayes; of wch the least
Is this, wth wch we celebrate yor feast.

124. horne-Musique] the music of horns—such as bugles, as well as the sowgelders' horns; pun on the horns of a cuckold.

137. drew] withdrew.

144. forward] eager.

149. vncouth Pollicie] unpleasant and evil plan or contrivance.

Enter the Masquers. A Lawyer wth stagges hornes
followed by a Courtier. A Countrey Chuffe wth
Rammes hornes, & a Souldier. An Vsurer wth
Goates hornes, & a Scholler. A spruce Cittizen
wth Oxe hornes, & a Butcher.

Tes. A speciall drove of horn-beasts! Wee'll see all.
Mer. These few are thought enough to shew, how more
Would appeare horrible. The Towne has store.
The first's a Lawyer, that by strife preuaild [8^{r}]
To wed a wife, that was by Loue intaild
Vnto a Courtier; who had the happe,
Soone after, to adorne him wth that Cappe.
The next a Countrey Cormorant, whose great wealth,
By a bad Fathers will, obtaind, by stealth,
A valiant Souldiers Mistres: For wch matter
This Enginiere wth Rammes his sconse did batter.
This an old gotish Vsurer, that must
Needs buy a Wretches Daughter to his Lust;
Doated, & married her wthout a Groat
This Herald gaue that crest vnto his Coat.
And that's the Cittizen, soe broadly pated;
W^{ch} the mad Butcher Cuckold-antidated.
Tes. They are a delicate damnable crew; and thou
An Anti-Mercury Prologuutor to
The devills.
Mer. Yo^{u} are much about the right S^{r}.
Now, by this daunce, let Husband, that doth wed,
Bride from her proper Loue to loathed bed,

153. *Chuffe*] miser.

160. by strife] by force, in connection with a legal dispute.

161. intaild] entail, the succession of property ownership; i.e., she loved a courtier.

164. Cormorant] "An insatiably greedy or rapacious person" (*OED*).

167. Enginiere] in military use, one who operates the "engines" of war or designs an attack.

167. Rammes] battering rams, or implements to break down the gates of a fort; ram horns of the cuckold.

167. sconse] fort built to defend something; skull.

170. Groat] English coin, not issued after 1662, which was approximately equal to four pence.

171. Coat] coat of arms; also the coat of the costume.

172. broadly pated] having a wide head, because of the ox horns.

173. Cuckold-antidated] made a cuckold before the ceremony.

174. delicate] effeminate; charming, used ironically.

175. Anti-Mercury] most probably, a devil as opposed to a god.

175. Prologuutor] prologuer, one who reads the prologue.

Observe his Fortune. Musique! Strike alowd
The Cuckolds Ioy, wth merry pipe & crowd.
Here they daunce to Musique of Violins & Cornets
The daunce ended, the Masquers goe off sodainly.
Tes. How now! All vanisht? The deuill take ye hindmost.
Quic. The foremost, I say; and lay him a block
For all the rest to breake theyr necks vpon.
Tes. Who are they? Can you guesse?
Mil. Truly not I Sr.
Vnlesse some of my husbands frends, that came
To warne him of his Fortune
Quic. Well considerd.
Tes. Why were not the dores shut vntill we knew 'hem?
Buz. They tooke an open course for that Sr wth a strong
Guard to maintaine theyr Egresse & their Degresse.
Mil. Shut 'hem fast after 'hem then; and let's to bed Chick;
And lock orselfes vp safe.
Quic. Yes: weell to bed since you will haue it soe.
This key shall be yor Guard: And here's another
For me. My house has store of beds in it
I brought you not to an vnfurnisht dwelling
Mil. But be not affraid to lye wth me good man.
I'll soe restore thee wth Cawdells & Cockbrothes;
Soe cuckle thee vp to morrow, thou shalt see
Quic. O Impudence.
Tes. I am quite out of my witts; and yet I'll councell
Thee Nephue
Buz. It is like to be mad Councell.

181. crowd] fiddle.

183. Glenn H. Blayney suggests that the wives in the masque love their husbands, despite having been forced to wed ("Enforcement of Marriage in English Drama," 467); his reading, however, is mistaken: the wives have cuckolded their husbands.

184. The deuill take ye hindmost] Tilley, D267; in medieval magic, the devil was said to have a school in which students ran down a passage and the slowest student was grabbed by the devil and was made his imp (Ebenezer C. Brewer, *Dictionary of Phrase and Fable*, 315).

185–86. lay . . . vpon] i.e., make him the block for the rest to fall over and break their necks; Tilley, B454.

193. open course] course of action that allowed them free access.

202. Cawdells] caudle, a "warm drink given to sick people, consisting of thin gruel, mixed with wine or ale sweetened and spiced" (Onions).

202. Cockbrothes] cockbroth, the broth of a boiled rooster; probable pun on "cock" as penis (Partridge).

203. cuckle thee vp] here, appears to mean "nourish" or "fondle"; see "cockle" (*OED*); pun on cuckold.

Mil. But will yo^{u} not ly wth me then?
Tes. Noe marry shall he not. Nephue yo^{u} shall not
Till shee can bride it modestly. Tis now
Too late: But I'll soe ratle her vp to morrow
Buz. Tis too late now; and yet hee'll doe't to morrow.
Tes. Goe. Will yo^{u} to yor Lodging?
Mil. Where be my bridemayds.
Where be the Batchelo^{r}s to disapoint my husband
Quic. Doe yo^{u} marke that?
Mil. I meane to take yor points. But yo^{u} haue none
O thrifty age! My husband is soe wise
To saue his points & hazard hookes & eyes.
Buz. She meanes the eyes in's head: I'll hang else.
My Master is like to haue a blind match on't. [8^{v}]
Tes. Take vp the lights Sirah.
Quic. I hope she talkes idly but for want of Sleepe.
And sleepe she shall for me to night.
Tes. And well sayd Nephue. To yor Chamber mistris.
Mil. Heigho heigho, to bed to bed to bed
Noe Bride soe glad—to keepe her Maydenhead. *Ex^{t} oẽs*

Finis Actus primi

Act. ii. Scœne i.

Lucy. Phillis.

Phillis like a Chambermayd

Lu. Y'are the first Mayd, that ere I entertain'd
Vpon soe small acquaintance. Yet y'are wellcome.

211. ratle her vp] scold her, or shake her, until she behaves.

215. disapoint my husband] i.e., disappoint him by preceding him in the marital bed.

217. take yor points] Points were the laces or cords of "twisted yarn, silk, or leather, for attaching the hose to the doublet, lacing a bodice, and fastening various parts where buttons are now used" (*OED*); thus, the "batchelors . . . to take yor points" would be the groomsmen to help him undress and prepare for the marital bed; possible puns on "getting pointers" from him and on measuring the points (tips) of a deer's antlers (horns of a cuckold).

221. blind match] a match with problems he did not foresee; or, a match of deceit. Cf. "A jealous man's horns hang in his eyes" (Tilley, M465).

226. Heigho] "An exclamation usually expressing yawning, sighing, languor, weariness, disappointment" (*OED*); Millicent may be wearied, but she is also pleased with her success—perhaps only the last line is an aside to the audience.

227. *Oẽs*] abbreviation of the Latin *omnes*, "all."

Act. ii. Scene i

4. entertain'd] entertained the services of, hired.

I like yor hand & cariage.
Ph. Tis yor fauour.
But Loue (they say) sweet mistres, is receau'd
At the first sight; and why not Service then,
Wch often brings more absolute returnes
Of the deare trust impos'd, & firmer faith
By Servants, then by Louers?
Lu. Stay there.
I may, by that, coniecture you haue bene
Deceau'd by some false Louer.
Ph. Who I Mistres?
I hope I looke to merily for such a one
And much too coursly too, to be belou d.
If I were sad & handsome, then it might
Be thought I were alitle Loue-sick. Pray
How long has this disease affected you?
This Melancholly Mistres? Not ere since
You lost yor father I hope.
Lu. For the most part.
Thou saydst (me thought) that Loue might be tane in
At the first sight.
Ph. There tis. She trod vpon
My corne eene now; and now I haue pinch'd hers
Loue, mistres? Yes. A mayd may take in more
Loue at one Looke, or one litle Loop-hole,
Then all the Doddy-polls in a Countrey can
Purge out on her while shee liues. Tis not to be
Cur'd by the Antimoniall cuppe; I meane
Shee smothring it, & not make knowne her passion.
Lu. Suppose shee loue an Enemy to her house
Ph. I haue found her fully. And suppose sweet Mistres
You be the loving woman, and young *Arthure*
(Whose Father was yor fathers Enemy)

7. fauour] friendly regard.

19. sad] sober, as opposed to "merily" in line 17.

27–28. She . . . hers] "You touch on the sore toe" (Tilley, T373).

30. Loop-hole] opening; vaginal entrance.

31. Doddy-polls] blockheads; *The Wisdome of Dr. Dodypoll* was a popular comedy at the turn of the century, and "dodypoll" was often used, as here, to mean a foolish doctor.

33. Antimoniall cuppe] "made of glass of antimony, to communicate emetic qualities to wine" (*OED*); the cure is in spilling forth her feelings, not hiding them.

Is yor belou'd—
Lu. I pray thee now, noe more
Phil. Now I haue struck the veine. Suppose I say [9^{r}]
All this were true: would yo^{u} confound yo^{r}selfe
In smothering yor Loue, (wch in itselfe
Is pure & innocent) vntill it grow
To a pernicious disease wthin yo^{u};
And hide it in yor bosome, till it worke
Yo^{r} kindled heart to ashes?
Lu. But canst thou find, or thinck it honorable
In me to foster such affection?
Ph. Yes; and religious; and most commendable,
Could yo^{u} but winne his Loue into a Mariage,
To beget peace betwixt yor Families.
How many, & what great examples haue we,
From former Ages, & of later times,
Of strong dissentions betweene furious Factions,
W^{ch} to their opposite houses haue drawne in
Eithers Allyes & Frends; whole Provinces;
Yea Kingdomes into deadly opposition,
Till the wide woundes on both sides haue sent forth
Riuers of blood; wch onely haue bene stopt
By the soft bands of Loue, in Mariages
Of equall branches sprung from the first Roots
Of all those hellbred hatreds?
Lu. My good Mayd—
Ph. Yes: I haue bene a good one to my griefe.
Lu. I loue that worthy Gentleman; and am confident,
That, in the time of o^{r} two fathers frendship,
He affected me noe lesse: But, since that time,
I haue not seene him, nor dare mention him,
To wrong my brothers patience; who is soe passionate,
That, could he but suspect I held a thought,
That fauourd him, I were foreuer lost.
For this sad cause, as well as for the losse
Of my deare Father, I haue sighd away
Twelue Moones in silent sorow; and haue heard,
That *Arthure* too (But for what cause I know not)

42. confound] destroy.
65. A reference to her previous "service" as Nat's maid-servant and mistress. See III.iv.56.

Has not bene seene abroad; but spends his time
In pensiue solitude.
Ph. Perhaps he grieues
As much for the supposed losse of yo^{u}
As of his father too.
Lu. The best construction,
I make of his retirdnes, is the blest
Prevention (wch I dayly pray for) of
A fatall meeting, twixt him & my brother;
W^{ch} would be sure the death of one, or both.
And now that feare invades me (as it dos allwayes)
My brother being absent whome I haue not seene
Since yesterday.
Ph. Feare nothing mistres. Now yo^{u} haue easd yor mind
Let me alone to comfort yo^{u}. And see, yor brother. *Ent: Theoph*
The. How is it wth yo^{u} Sister?
Lu. Much better now, then when yo^{u} left me brother
But why looke yo^{u} soe sadly? Speake deare brother.
I hope yo^{u} did not meet the Man yo^{u} hate
If yo^{u} did, speake; If yo^{u} haue fought & slaine him,
I chardge yo^{u} tell me, that I may know the worst
Of Fortune can befall me. I shall gaine [9^{v}]
Perhaps a death by't. Therefore pray yo^{u} tell me
The. Yo^{u} speake as if yo^{u} lou'd the Man I hate
And that yo^{u} feare I haue killd him
Ph. Not for loue
Of him (I assure yo^{u} S^{r}.) but of yo^{r}selfe.
Her feare in this case, s^{r}, is that the Law
May take from her the comfort of her Life
In taking yo^{u} from her; and soe shee were
But a dead woman. We were speaking
Of such a danger iust as yo^{u} came in.
And truly S^{r} my heart eene tremble trembles
To thinck vpon it yet. Pray S^{r} resolue her.

88. absent] absent) *MS*. The parenthesis could provide a semantic signal, but it is omitted here both because it is syntactically confusing and because the first stroke of the following "w" partially covers it, indicating that the writer may have meant to omit it. 91. SD *Theoph*] *runs off the page MS*.

85. fatall] deadly; inevitable, should both be abroad.

The. Then twas yor friuolous feare that wrought in her.
Good Sister be at peace: For by my Loue to yo^{u}
(An oath I will not violate) I neither saw
Nor sought him I. But other thoughts perplexe me
Lu. Indeed yor stay all night was fearefull to me.
What! Were yo^{u} at the Wedding brother?
The. Whose Wedding Sister?
Lu. Yo^{r} lost Loue *Millicents*. Are yo^{u} now sad
After yor last leaue taking?
There may be other matches my deare brother.
The. Yo^{u} wrong me shamefully to thinck, that I
Can thinck of other, then her Memory.
Though shee be lost & dead to me, can yo^{u}
Be soe vnnaturall, as to desire
The seperation of a thought of mine
From her deare Memory; wch is all the comfort
My heart is maried to, or I can liue by.
Ph. Surely, good S^{r}, in my opinion
Sharpe eager stomachs may be better fed
Wth th'aiery smell of meat, then the bare thought
Of the most curious dainties.
The. What peece of impudence haue yo^{u} receau'd
Into my house to vexe my patience?
Lu. Pray brother pardon me. I tooke her, as
I find her, for my comfort. Shee has wrought
By councell & discourse into my thoughts
Much ease, & some delight.
The. Good mayd forgiue mee.
And gentle Sister beare wth my destractions.
Ph. A good natur'd gentleman for all his fiery flashes.
The. And now I'll tell yo^{u} Sister (doe not chide me)
I haue a new Affliction
Lu. What ist brother?
The. I am ingag'd vnto a Gentleman,
(A noble valiant Gentleman) for my life.
(For ought I know) by hazarding his owne
In my behalfe.
Lu. It was gainst *Arthure* then.

123. Though] Thou *MS.* 130. aiery] "i" *interlined MS.*

What Villaine wast, durst take yor cause in hand
Against that man?
The. You wrong me beyond suffrance
And my deare Fathers blood wthin yo^{u}, to seeme carefull
Of that mans safty.
Ph. His safty S^{r}? Alasse
She meanes he is a Villaine that would take
The honor of his death out of yor hands
If he must fall by sword of man.
The. Againe I aske yor pardon. But I had [10^{r}]
A quarrell yesterday, that drew strong ods
Vpon my single person: Three to one
When, at the instant, that braue Gentleman
That Mars of men, whome I began to mention,
Wth his Sword sides me, and putts'hem all to flight
Lu. But how can that afflict yo^{u}.
The. My affliction is
That I not know the man, to whome I am
Soe much ingag'd, to giue him thanks at least *Ent: Nathaniell.*
O S^{r}! Yo^{u} now are wellcome; though weꝑted
Abruptly yesterday.
Nat. I thanck yo^{u} S^{r}.
The. 'Pray thee *Nat* tell me (I hope (at least) thou knowst him)
What Gentleman was that, came in betwixt vs?
Nat If the deuill know him noe better, he will loose
A part of's due I thinck. But to the purpose
I knew yo^{u} would be frends before I came:
How-ere I haue a newes that may deserue
Yo^{r} Loue, though now yo^{u} were my deadly Enemy
The. What is it *Nat*?
Nat. Sweet m^{r}s *Lucy*—
[*Lu.*] My brother attends yor newes.
Nat. My wench become her Chambermayd! Very pretty!
How the Iade mumps, for I should discouer her.

171. him)] him *MS.* 180. *Lu.*] *The. MS.*

173–74. If . . . due] "Give the devil his due" (Tilley, D273).

179. The SD in *O* indicates that Nat kisses her hello.

182. for I should discouer her] i.e., for fear her relationship with Nat will be exposed. The word "fear" may have been omitted accidentally from the manuscript; it appears in *O*.

The. Yo^{r} newes good *Nat*? What, is it ready made?
Or are yo^{u} now but coyning it?
Nat. Noe it was coynd last night; of the right stamp too.
And passes current for yor good. Now know
That I & *Mun*, & *Vince*, & diuers others
Of o^{r} Camrades were last night at the Bride-house
The. What mischiefe did yo^{u} there?
Nat. A Masque, a Masque, Lad, in wch we p^{r}sented
The Miseries of inforc'd Mariages
Soe liuely—Zookes lay by yor captious countenance
And heare me handsomely
Lu. Good brother doe. It has a fine beginning
Nat. But marke what followes.
This morning, early, vp we got againe
And wth o^{r} Fidlers made a fresh assalt
And battry gainst the bedrid bridegroomes window
Wth an old Song (a very wondrous ould one)
Of all the cares, vexations, feares, & torments
That a decrepid, nasty, rotten husband
Meets in a youthfull, beauteous sprightly bride:
Soe, as the weake old wretch will shortly feare,
That his owne feebler shadow makes him Cuckold.
Our Masque ore night begat a seperation
Betwixt'hem before bed-time: For we found
Him, at one window, coughing & spitting at vs;
She, at another, laughing & throwing money
Downe to the Fids; while her old Vncle *Testy*,
From a third Port-hole, raues, denouncing Law
And thondring statutes gainst their Minstralsy.
Lu. Would he refuse his Bride-bed
Phil. Marry hang him.
Nat Our horne-masque pusht him off it (blesse my Invention)
For wch I thinck yo^{u}'ll Iudge shee'll forsake him

184. coyning] creating; minting; engendering, as with a child.

185. stamp] kind, sort; the die used to imprint coins; parentage.

186. passes current] is generally accepted as being; is accepted as currency.

191. Possibly a reference to George Wilkins, *The Miseries of Enforced Marriage* (3d quarto, 1629; 4th quarto, 1637).

193. handsomely] courteously.

210. denouncing] proclaiming, "in the manner of a threat or warning" (*OED*).

211. statutes . . . Minstralsy] likely the laws regarding disturbance of the peace.

214. pusht him off it] i.e., cooled his ardor.

214. Invention] the plan; his powers of inventiveness.

All nights & dayes hereafter. Here's a blessing
Prepard, now, for yo^{u}, if yo^{u} haue grace to follow't.
The. Out of my house; That I may kill thee. Goe [10^{v}]
For here it were inhospitable. Hence
Thou busy Villayne, that wth sugard Malice
Hast poyson'd all my hopes; ruin'd my Comforts
In that sweet Soule foreuer. Goe I say, that I may kill thee
Nat. Is this yor way of thancks for curtesies?
Or ist our luck allwayes to meet good frends
And neuer part soe? Yet, before I goe,
I will demand yor Reason (if yo^{u} haue any)
Wherein o^{r} frendly care can p^{r}iudice yo^{u}
Or poison any hopes of yo^{r}s in *Millicent*?
Lu. Pray brother tell him
The. Yes that he may dy satisfied, I did but Iustice
In killing him. That Villaine old in Mishiefe
(Hell take him) that has married her, conceaues
It was my plot. I know he dos. And for a sure
Reuenge will eyther worke her death
By poison or some other subtle crueltie;
Or keepe her lockt vp in such Miserie
That I shall neuer see her more
Nat. S^{r} I can answere yo^{u}
The. Not in a word. Let me intreat yo^{u} goe
Nat. Faire m^{r}s *Lucy*—
The. Neither shall she heare yo^{u}.
Nat. Her mayd shall heare me then; or I'll not out
To night.
Phil. Pray S^{r}, on what acquaintance.
Nat. Be not affraid. I take noe notice on thee
I like thy course wench, & will keepe thy councell.
And come sometimes & bring thee a bitt
Phil. I'll see yo^{u} chok'd first.
Nat. Thou art not the first
Cast wench, that has made a good Chambermayd

218. *The.*] *The. Nat.* ("*Nat.*" *deleted*) *MS*. "*Nat*" is also the catchword at the bottom of 10^{r}.
222. may kill thee] may / kill thee *MS*. "Kill thee" is written below "I may" as a runover.

220. busy] meddlesome. Cf. "busybody."
247. a bitt] a "bit" of sex; small coin, to pay for sex; the bit of a bridle, with reference to sexual riding (?).

Though I would allmost ha'sworne thou hadst bene free
And set vp for thy selfe before this time.
Phil. O yo^{u} are base: and I could claw yor eyes out.
Nat. I, but for loosing thy place *Phil.* *Ex^{t}.*
Lu. Brother I thanck yo^{u} that yo^{u} promise me
Yo^{u} will not follow him now. What wast he sayd
To yo^{u} *Phillis*?
Phil. Helpe me good Apron strings.
The. What was't he sayd?
Phil. Marry he sayd in answere of yor obiections
First that whereas yo^{u} feard that the old man
Would worcke his faire wiues death; That is not
To be feard, while she has soe much feare
Of Heauen before her Eyes. Next, that whereas
Yo^{u} doubt hee'll lock her vp from sight of man
He sayes shees soe indued wth witt of woman
That were she lockd, or had locks hung vpon her;
Locks vpon Locks; Locks of Preuention
Locks of Security, yet as shee is a woman
She would haue her will, & breake all those Locks
As easily as her Wed-lock.
Lu. Did he say soe?
Phi. Yes that he did forsooth.
Lastly, for yor accesse vnto her sight,
If yo^{u} haue Land (he sayes) to sell or Mortgage
Hee'll vndertake, his dores, his wife & all
Shall fly wide open to yo^{u}.
Lu: He could not say soe [11^{r}]

270. all] *interlined with a caret MS.* 270. Locks] Locks as easily ("as easily" *deleted*) *MS.*

251–52. free . . . selfe] become a prostitute; the term comes from the idea of being made "free" of a company or guild, i.e., admitted to it and allowed to work.

258. Apron strings] "A woman needs but to look on her apron string to find an excuse" (Tilley, W659).

262–64. That . . . Eyes.] In Millicent's virtue lies her safety: Quicksands would not risk the consequences, earthly or divine, of killing so pious a woman; nor would he be revenged on Millicent or Theophilus by sending Millicent's soul to heaven.

266. indued] endowed.

267. locks hung vpon her] perhaps a reference to a chastity belt.

269–70. as . . . will] Tilley, W723; probably also an allusion to William Haughton's *Englishmen for My Money; or, A Woman Will Have Her Will* (c. 1598), in which three daughters, locked in the house by their usurer father, nonetheless manage to marry the men they love. The play was popular—a third quarto was printed in 1631, a few years before *The English Moor* was composed.

276. vndertake] assert.

The. 'Troth, but tis like his wild way of expression.
I must be frends wth him.
Lu. That's well said brother. *Ent: Arnold.*
The. Now *Arnold*! Any tidings
Ar. Not of the Gentleman I sought, that fought for yo^{u}.
I could by noe meanes find him.
The. He was the brauest fellow Sister.
Ar. But I haue other newes thats worth yor notice
To p^{r}vent mischiefe
The. What's that?
Ar. Yo^{r} Enemy, young *Arthure*, that has not beene
Seene abroad this Twellmonth, is now got forth,
In a disguise, I heare, & soundly arm'd.
I haue it from most sure Intelligence
Looke to yo^{r}selfe S^{r}.
Lu. Now my blood chills agen.
The. Pseugh; I'll not thinck of him. Let's in to breakfast. *Ex^{t} oẽs*

Scene. ii. Quicksands. Testy. Millicent.

Qu. Here was a good night & a good-morrow too
Giuen by a crew of devills wth a Mischiefe!
Tes. It was her villanous plot, & she shall smart fort.
If I may councell yo^{u}.
Mil. Smart did yo^{u} say
I thinck tis smart enough for a Young bride
To be made lye alone & gnaw the sheets
Vpon her wedding night.
Tes. Rare Impudence!
Mil. But, for yor satisfaction, as I hope
To gaine yor fauour, cause yo^{u} are my Vncle,
I know not any Actor in this busines.
Though I perswade my selfe they are of those
That stile themselfes my frends.
Qui. How now! *Ent: Buzzard.*
Buz. S^{r} here's a Letter throwne into the entry *Ex^{t}.*

286. thats] that *MS*; thats *O*. (A comma after "newes" would also clarify the line in *MS*.)

295. Pseugh] pshaw.

Tes. It is some villanous Libell then I warrant
Qui. Pray read it S^{r}. Not mine owne house free from hem?
The devill out me a spight: And, when he has ploughd
An old mans lust vp, he sitts girning at him.
Mil. May I be worthy S^{r} to know what trobles yo^{u}?
Qui. Doe yo^{u} know yo^{r}selfe?
Mil. Am I yor troble then.
Qui. Tis sworne, & written there thou shalt be wicked:
Hundreds, that envy me haue tane their oathes,
To make thee false, & me a horned Monster.
Mil. And dos that trouble yo^{u}?
Qui. Dos it not yo^{u}?
Mil. A dreame has done much more
And now S^{r} I'll be serious; and will offer
To mend yor faith in mee. Ist in theyr power
To destroy vertue thinck yo^{u}? or doe yo^{u}
Suppose mee false allready? Tis perhaps
Theyr plot to driue yo^{u} into that opinion,
And soe to make yo^{u} cast me out among'hem.
Yo^{u} may doe soe vpon the words of strangers
And if they tell yo^{u} all yor gold is counterfet
Throw that out after mee.
Tes. Now shee speakes woman
Mil. But since these men p^{r}tend; and yo^{u} suppose'hem
To be my frends, that carry this p^{r}sumption [11^{v}]
Ouer my will, I'll take chardge of my selfe;
And doe faire Iustice both on them & yo^{u}.
My honor is mine owne; and I am noe more
Yo^{r}s yet (on whome mine Vncle has bestowd me)
Then all the worlds (the Ceremony off)
And will remaine soe, free from them & yo^{u},

39. Throw] Through ("ugh" *deleted and* "w" *interlined with a caret*) *MS*.

20. The devill out me a spight] "The devil owed him a shame and now he has paid it" (Tilley, D261).

21. girning] showing teeth in a snarl; grinning.

27. horned Monster] cuckold.

40. speakes woman] i.e., speaks as a good woman should.

47. (the Ceremony off)] excluding the ceremony; since they have not consummated the marriage, she says, she belongs to him no more than to anyone else.

That by the false light of their wild fire flashes
Haue slighted & deprau'd me & yor bride-bed,
Till yo^{u} recant yor willfull Ignorance,
And they their petulant follies.
Tes. This sounds well.
Mil. Both they & yo^{u} trench on my peace & honor,
Dearer then Beauty, Pleasure, Wealth & Fortune.
I'ld stand vnder the fall of mine Estate
Most chearefully, & Sing: For there be wayes
To raise vp Fortunes ruines, were her towers
Shatterd in peeces; and the glorious ball
Shee stands on cleft asunder. But for Peace
Once ruin'd there's noe reparation.
If Honor fall (wch is the Soule of Life)
Tis like the damned, it nere lifts the head
Vp to the light agen.
Tes. Neece thou hast wonne me;
And Nephue, Shee's to good for yo^{u}: And I chardge yo^{u}
Giue her her will, I'll haue her home agen else.
Qui. I know not what I can deny her now.
Mil. I aske but this. That yo^{u} will giue me leaue
To keepe a vow I made, wch was last night
Because yo^{u} slighted me—
Tes. Stay there alitle.
I'll lay the price of ten mayden-heads now
(As the Market goes) yo^{u} get not hers this Sẽnight.
Mil. My vow is for a Month; and for soe long
I craue his faithfull promise not to attempt me.
In the meane time, becaus I will be quit
Wth my trim forward Gentlemen, & secure yo^{u}
From their assaults, let it be giuen out,
That yo^{u} haue sent me downe into the Countrey,

76. not] t not ("t" *deleted*) *MS.*

49. false light] unreal light, as opposed to that of the sun; false impression created, in the sense of viewing someone or something in a "false light."

49. wild fire flashes] flashes of lightning; outrageous, quick, and empty phrases. Cf. Jonson, *Eastward Hoe*, IV.ii.254–55: "I am sory to see such flashes as these proceede from a Gentleman of your Quality" (*OED*).

54. trench on] encroach upon, endanger.

77. quit] even with, in the sense of retaliation; rid of.

78. forward] presumptuous.

Or back vnto my Vncles, whether yo^{u} please.
Qui. Or tarry tarry; Stay stay here awhile.
Mil. Soe I intend S^{r}. I'll not leaue yor house;
But be lockd vp in some convenient roome,
Not to be seene by any but yo^{r}selfe;
Or else to haue the Libertie of yor house
In some disguise (if it were possible)
Free from the least suspition of yor Servants.
Quic. I vnderstand her drift S^{r}, & applaud
Her queint devise. We shall agree I see
Tes. Agree on't betwixt yo^{r}selfes. I see y'are frends.
I must away downe to my countrey house
Now I dare trust thee Neece. Comply still wth him.
He is in yeares, tis true. But dost thou heare me?
Old Foxes are best blades
Mil. I'm sure they stinck most
Tes. Good keeping makes him bright & young againe
Mil. But for how long?
Tes. A yeare, or two perhaps.
Then, when he dyes, his wealth makes thee a Countesse.
Mil. Yo^{u} speake much comfort S^{r}.
Tes. That's my good girle.
And, Nephue, Loue her. I find shee deserves it.
Be as benevolent to her as yo^{u} can. [12^{r}]
Shew yor good will at least: Yo^{u} doe not know
How the good-will of an old man may worke,
In a young wife. I must away I say.
At a monthes end I'll visit yo^{u} againe
Ioy & content be wth yo^{u}.
Amb. And a good Iourney to yo^{u}. *(Ex^{t} Testy.*
Qui. Yo^{u} are content, yo^{u} say, to be lockt vp,
Or put in some disguise, and haue it sayd
Yo^{u} are gone vnto yor Vncles. I haue heard
Of some bridegroomes, that shortly after Mariage

94. me?] me,? *MS.*

90. queint devise] clever plan.

95. Foxes] A fox was "a kind of sword. . . . It has been conjectured that this use arose from the figure of a wolf, on certain sword-blades, being mistaken for a fox" (*OED*); cunning men.

95. blades] general term for swords, deriving from the cutting edge, or blade; gallants, as in "gay blades"; lovers, from the idea of penis as sword.

96. Millicent deliberately plays on the meaning of "old foxes" as "aging animals."

110. *Amb.*] abbreviation of the Latin *ambo*, "both."

Haue gone to see their Vncles, seldome Brides:
They are not soe quickly weary of theyr houses.
I haue thought of another course.
Mil. Be it any way.
Qui. What if it were giuen out yo^{u} are run away?
(Out of a detestation of yor Match)
Absolutely run away?
Mil. Twould pull a blot
Vpon my reputation, that.
Qui. Noe noe.
When they consider my vnworthines
Twill giue it credit. All will comend yo^{u} for't.
Mil. Yo^{u} speake well for yo^{r}selfe.
Qui. I speake as they'll speake.
Mil. Well, let it be soe then. I am content.
Qui. Wee'll put this instantly in act. The rest,
As for disguise, or priuacy in my house
You'll leaue to me?
Mil. All S^{r} to yor dispose.
Provided still yo^{u} vrge not to infringe
My vow concerning my virginity
Qui. Tis the least thing I thinck on.
By my Life, Wealth & Fortune, all I haue,
I will not offer at it till yor owne time
Mil. Why here's a happines in a husband now. *Ex^{t}.*

Scene iii. Dionisia. Rafe.

Dio. Thou tellst me things, that Truth neuer came neare.
Impossible as Fates prevention.
Ra: Tis perfect truth
Dio. Mayntayn't but in one sillable
I'll teare thy mischeiuous tongue out
Ra: A fit reward for telltruthes.
But that's not the reward yo^{u} promis'd me

125. When] Twill When ("Twill" *deleted*) *MS.*

116. Most brides would be excited about their new possessions and position of authority—too excited to leave soon. Aside from marriage, women in general had few options beyond dependency and the nunnery (Maurice Ashley, "Love and Marriage in Seventeenth-Century England," 671).

To watch & sift yor brothers actions
And bring yo^{u} the account. Yo^{u} said forsooth
(If't please yo^{u} to remember) yo^{u} would loue me.
Dio. I bid thee bring account of what he did
Against his Enemy, and thou reportst
He tooke his Enemyes danger on himselfe;
And holpe to rescue him, whose merciles Father
Was the vntimely end of ours. Can Truth
Or common Reason claime a part in this report?
Ra. Tis not for any spight I owe my Master
But for my itch at her, that I doe this.
I am strangely taken. Such braue spirited women
Haue cherishd strong-backd servingmen ere now
Dio. Why dost not get thee from my sight false fellow
Ra. I'll be beleeu'd first. Therefore haue but patience
To peruse that. *(a paper*
Dio. My brothers Character.
Theophilus sisters name—the brighter *Lucy*.
Soe often written? Nothing but her name? [12^{v}]
But change of Attributes—One serves not twise.
Blessed, Divine, Illustrious, all Perfection—
And (soe heauen blesse me) powerfull, in one place.
The worst thing I read yet, heape of all Vertues—
Bright shining—and all these ascrib'd to *Lucy*.
O, I could curse thee now for being soe iust.
Would thou hadst belyed him still.
Ra. I nere bely'd him I.
But since yo^{u} are soe displeasd wth what I thought
Would haue bene gratefull service to yo^{u}, I wish
I had not bene so busy in it.
Dio. O mischiefe of affection! Monstrous! horrid!
It shall not passe soe quietly. Nay stay.
Ra. Shee'll cut my throat I feare.
Dio. Thou art a faithfull Servant
Ra. It may doe yet.
Dio. How I doe loue thee now!

19. itch] itch I ("I" *deleted*) *MS*.

9. sift] closely question; "scrutinize narrowly, so as to find out the truth" (*OED*).

20. braue] courageous; handsome.

25. Character] handwriting.

Ra. And yor Loue Mistres
Braue sprightly Mistres, is the steeple top,
Or rather Weather-cock on top of that,
To wch aspires my Lifes ambition.
Dio. How didst thou get this paper?
Ra. Amongst many
Of his rare twell'months melancholly workes
That lye in his study. Mistres, tis apparant
His Melancholly all this while has bene
More for her Loue then for his fathers death.
Dio. Thou hast my Loue foreuer.
Ra. Some small token
In earnest of it, Mistres, would be felt.
Dio. Take that in earnest then. *(She strikes him*
Ra. It is a sure one
And the most feeling pledge shee could haue giuen:
For shee is a Virago. And I haue read
That yor Viragos vse to strike all those
They meane to lye wth. And from thence tis taken
That yor braue actiue women are calld strikers.
Dio. Set me that chayre. *(She sitts*
Ra. Shee's mine. Here's a good place for't Mistres.
Wthin *Arthure.* Sister where are yo^{u}?
Ra. Devill! I am prevented.
Dio. Away. My brother comes. But still be sure
I loue thee
Ra: Ah ha! Another time I am sure on't. *Ex^{t}. Ent: Arthure*
Art. Sister! How now! not well? or sleepy?
Dio. O brother—Sick sick brother. Sick at heart
Ar. Passion of heart! Where are o^{r} Servants now
To run for doctors? hoe!

64. braue] braue spiritted ("spiritted" *deleted*) *MS*.

51. rare] unusual, exceptional; sometimes used ironically.

57. The SD in *O* reads: "*He offers to kiss her, she strikes him.*"

61. Virago] vigorous, bold woman, often with the connotation of impudence.

64. strikers] persons who easily resort to blows; fornicators. Cf. Glapthorne, *Lady Mother*, IV.i: "These are immodest devills that make modest ladyes become strickers" (*OED*).

66. for't] The reference may be to the chair, in which case the SD is simply at the wrong line, but the reference also may be to the action Rafe hopes will take place.

75. Passion of heart] heart disease; love.

Dio. Pray stay, & heare me
Here's noe worke for them. They'll find a Master, here,
To powerfull for the strength of all their knowledge
Ar. What at thy heart?
Dio. Yes brother, at my heart,
To scornefull to be dispossest by them
Ar. What may that prowd griefe be? dear sister name it.
Dio. It grieues me more to name it, then to suffer it.
Since I haue indur'd the worst on't, and prou'd constant
To sufferance & silence, 'twere a weaknes
Now to betray a Sorrow by a name
More fit to be seuerely felt then knowne
Ar. Indeed I'll know't. [13^{r}]
Dio. Yet rather let me dy,
Then soe afflict yor vnderstanding S^{r}.
Ar. It shall not afflict me.
Dio. I know you'll chide me for't.
Ar. Indeed yo^{u} wrong me now. Can I chide yo^{u}?
Dio. If yo^{u} be true & honest yo^{u} must doe it,
And heartily.
Ar. Yo^{u} taxe me nearly there.
Dio. And that's the phisick must helpe me, or nothing.
Ar. Wth griefe I goe about to cure a griefe then.
Now speake it boldly sister.
Dio. Noble Phisitian. It is--------------
Ar. It is—What is it? If yo^{u} loue me, speake.
Dio. Tis—Loue—And I beseech thee spare me not
Ar. Alasse deare Sister, canst thou thinck, that Loue
Deserves a chiding in a gentle breast
Dio. Doe yo^{u} pitty me allready? O faint man,
That trembles but at opening of a wound!
What hope is there of thee to search & dresse it?
But I am in thy hands, & forc'd to try thee.
I loue-------------*Theophilus*
Ar. hah!
Dio. *Theophilus*, brother,
His Sonne, that slew o^{r} Father. There's a Loue!

83. griefe] disease or wound; mental pain.
106. faint] lacking courage.
108. search] probe the wound.

O more then time twere look'd too, feare it festers.
Ar. She has put me to't indeed. What must I doe? *(aside*
Shee has a violent spirit; Soe has hee;
And though I wish most seriously the match,
(Whereby to worke mine owne wth his faire Sister,)
The daunger, yet, in the Negotiation
May quite destroy my course, spoile all my hopes.
I'll therefore put her off on't if I can.
Dio. Can yo^{u} be tender now?
Ar. What to vndoe yo^{u}?
I loue yo^{u} not soe slightly. Pardon me
A rough hand must be vs'd: For here's a wound
Must not be gently touch'd; yo^{u} perish then
Vnder a brothers pitty. Pray sitt quiet:
For yo^{u} must suffer all.
Dio. I'll striue to doe it.
Ar. To loue the Sonne of him, that slew yor Father!
To say it shewes vnlovingnes of Nature;
Forgetfullnes in blood, were all but shallow
To the great depth of daunger yor fault stands in.
It rather iustifies the act it selfe;
And com̃ends that downe to Posteritie
By yor blood-cherishing embraces. Children
Borne of yor body, will in stead of teares,
By yor example, offer a thanckfull Ioy
To the sad memory of their Grandsires slaughter.
Quite contrary! How fearefull tis to thinck on't!
What may the world say too? There goes a daughter
Whose strange desire leapt from her Fathers ruine;
Death gaue her to the Bridegroome; and the Mariage
Knitt fast & cemented wth blood—O Sister—
Dio. O brother. *(She rises.*
Ar. How! Well? & soe quickly well?
Dio. Dissembler; Foule dissembler.
Ar. This is plaine.
[*Dio.*] Thou hast playd wth fire, and, like a cunning fellow, [13^{v}]

149. *Dio.*] *no speaker change MS.*

115. put me to't] i.e., put me in a difficult situation.
121. put her off on't] divert her from it, dissuade her.
142. strange] abnormal.

Bitt in thy paine, on purpose to deceaue
Anothers tender touch. I know thy heart weepes
For what't has spoke against. Thou that darst loue
The daughter of that fiend, that slew thy father,
And plead against thy cause. Vnfeeling man!
Cannot thy owne words melt thee? To that end
I wrought & raisd them. 'T was to winne thy health
That I was sick; I playd thy disease to thee,
That thou mightst see the loathd complection on't,
Farre truer in another, then ones selfe.
And, if thou canst after all this tread wickedly,
Thou art a Rebell to all naturall Loue,
And filiall duty; dead to all iust Councell;
And euery word, thou mockdst wth vehemence,
Will rise a wounded Father in thy Conscience,
To scourge thy Iudgement. There's thy Saint crost out
And all thy memory wth her. I'll nere trust
Reuenge againe wth thee; Soe false is Man-hood.
I'll take it now into mine owne power fully;
And see what I can doe, though wth Life's hazard.
Yo^{r} purpose shall nere thriue. There I'll make sure worke. *(Ex^{t}.*

Ar. How wise & cunning is a womans Malice!
I neuer was soe cossend. *Ex^{t}.*

Finis Actus Secundi.

Act. iii. Scœne i.

Quicksands. Buzzard. Madge.

Qui. Out of my dores, pernicious Knaue & Harlot.
Auaunt I say.
Buz. Good master
Ma. Pray yor worship.
Qui. Yo^{u} haue all the wages yo^{u} are like to haue
Buz. Nay I dare take yor word for that. You'll keepe
All moneyes fast enough, whose ere it be,
If yo^{u} but gripe it once.
Qui. I am vndone & sham'd foreuer by yor negligence;

158. complection on't] appearance of it.
165. There's thy Saint crost out] The SD in *O* reads: "She tears & throws the paper to him."

Or Malice rather: For how could it be
Shee could depart my house wthout yor knowledge?
Buz. If I knew of her flight Sr, may these hands
Neuer be held vp, but to curse you onely,
If you cashiere me thus.
Ma. And for my part,
Or ought I know, she may as well be gone
Out of the Chimney toppe, as out of dore.
Qui. The dore must be yor way; and find her out
Or neuer find my dore againe. Be gone
Amb. O you are a cruell Master *Ext Amb.*
Quic. Soe, soe, soe. [14r]
These cryes are Laughter to me. ha ha ha.
I will be master of my Invention once;
And now be bold to see how rich I am
In viewing of my wealth. * Come precious marke **Ent Millicent*
Of Beauty & Perfection, at wch Envy
And Lust ayme all their ranckling poysonous arrowes
But I'll provide they nere shall touch thy blood
Mil. What! are yor Servants gone?
Quic. Turn'd, turnd away for thy suppos'd escape,
Wch they will rumor soe to my disgrace
Abroad, that all my envious Adversaries
Will, betwixt Ioy of my conceau'd Misfortune
In thy deare Losse, & their vaine hopes to find thee
Run frantick through the streets; whilst we, at home,
Sit safe & laugh at their defeated Malice.
Mil. But now for my disguise?
Quic. I that, that, that.
Be but soe good & gentle to thy selfe
To heare me & be ruld by me in that,
A queenes felicitie falls short of thine.
I'll make thee Mistres of a Mine of Treasure
Giue me but peace the way that I desire it—
Mil. Some horrible shape sure that he coniures soe.
Quic. That I may foole Iniquity, & triumph
Ouer the Lustfull Stallions of or time;

25. Invention] plan.
27. marke] standard, target; possible pun on "mark" as money of account, generally valued at 160 pence.

Bed-bounders & Leap-Ladyes (as they terme'hem)
Mount-Mistresses: Diseases shackle'hem;
And Spittles pick their bones. I shake to thinck on'hem.
Mil. Come, to the point. What's the disguise I pray yo^{u}?
Qui. First know, my Sweet, it was the queint devise
Of a *Venetian* merchant, wch I learnt
In my young Factorship
Mil. That of the Moore?
The Blackamore yo^{u} spake of? Would yo^{u} make
A *Negro* of me?
Quic. Yo^{u} haue past yor word
That if I vrge not to infringe yor vow
For keeping this month yor virginity
You'll weare what shape I please. Now this shall both
Kill vaine attempts in me, and guard yo^{u} safe
From all that seeke subuersion of yor honor.
I'll feare noe powderd Spirits to haunt my house,
Rose-footed feinds, or fumigated Goblins
After this Tincture is layd vpon thy face.
Twill coole theyr Kidneys, & lay downe their heats.
Mil. Blesse me! yo^{u} fright me S^{r}. Can Iealousie
Creepe into such a shape? Would yo^{u} blot out
Heauens Workmanship?
Quic. Why, thinckst thou, fearefull Beauty,
Has Heauen noe part in *Egipt*? Pray thee tell me
Is not an *Ethiops* face his workmanship
As well as the fairst Ladyes? Nay more too
Then hers, that dawbes & makes adulterate beauty.
Some can be pleas'd to lie in oyles & paste
At Sinnes appointment, wch is thrice more wicked.
This (wch is sacred) is for Sinnes prevention.

51. Spittles] spitals, houses to receive the diseased, especially those "of a low class or afflicted with foul diseases" (*OED*).

55. Factorship] term of employment as a mercantile agent; a commission merchant.

65. powderd Spirits] the walking dead; men with powdered hair or perukes, gallants.

66. Rose-footed feinds] red, cloven-hooved devils; quiet, wicked men.

66. fumigated Goblins] demons from the smoke and fumes of Hell; evil, tobacco-smoking men.

67. Tincture] black coloring. Black paint was often used in masques and on the popular stage, allowing white persons to represent blackamoors. See Eldred D. Jones, "The Physical Representation of African Characters."

68. Kidneys] The kidneys were believed to receive the heated matter that was created when passion was aroused.

Illustrious Persons, nay euen Queenes themselfes
Haue, for the glory of a Nights presentment
To grace the worke, sufferd as much as this [14^{v}]
Mil. Enough S^{r}; I'm obedient
Qui. Now I thanck thee.
Be feareles Loue; this alters not thy beauty
Though for a time, obscures it from o^{r} eyes.
Thou mayst be white at pleasure: Like the Sun
Thou dost but case thy Splendor in a Clowd
To make the beame more precious when it shines.
Hold; take the tincture; and perfect what's amisse.
Mil. My habit, too, must off, & humbler be put on
Quic. Please yor owne fancy. Take my keyes of all.
In my pawne-wardrobe yo^{u} shall find to fit yo^{u}.
Mil. But S^{r} here's one thing much considerable;
That though I outwardly appeare yor drudge
Tis fit I haue a Mayd for priuate service.
My breeding has not bene to serve myselfe. *Ex^{t} Mil*
Quic. Trust to my care for that. One knocks. In In. *Enter Phillis*
Is it to me, yor busines? *like a Country Lasse*
Phi Yea, if yo^{u} be master *Quicksands*
The Masters worship of the house.
Qui. I am soe.
What's yor busines?
Phi. S^{r} and'ta like yor worship hoping that
You'll pardon my presumpsiousnes
I am a Mother, that doe lack a Service
Qui. Yo^{u} haue said enough. I'll entertaine no Mothers.
But a good Maid servant, knew I where to find one
Phi. He is a knaue, & like yor worship, that

108. no] to *MS.*

80–82. A reference to courtly participation in masques, such as Queen Anne's appearance as a blackamoor in Jonson's *Masque of Blackness* (1605). One wonders whether Brome was aware that William Seymour's first wife, Arabella Stuart, was one of the nymphs in that performance (Violet A. Wilson, *Society Women of Shakespeare's Time*, 184).

87–89. Cf. Prince Hal's speech in Shakespeare, *I Henry IV*, I.ii.191–97.

93. pawne-wardrobe] a wardrobe of clothes accepted as security by a pawnbroker.

107. Mother] Phillis uses "mawther," meaning an unmarried woman or a young girl in Norfolk dialect (Wright).

Dares say I am noe Maid; And for a Servant
(It ill becomes poore folke to praise themselfes)
But I were held a tidy one at home
Qui O, th'art a *Norfolke* Woman (Cry thee mercie)
Where Maids are Mothers, & Mothers are Mayds
Phi. S^r I haue frends i the Citty that will passe
Their words for my good bearing
Qui. Hast thou
Phi Yes S^r.
I haue a Cosin that is an Attorney
Of *Layons Inne*, that will not see me wrongd
And an old Aunt in *Muggle Street*, a Midwife
That knowes what's what as well as another woman.
Qui. But whereabout in *Norfolke* wer't thou bred?
Phi. At *Thripperstowne* S^r, neare the Citty of *Norwich*
Qui. Where they liue much by spinning wth the Rocks?
Phi. Thripping the call it S^r.
Qui. Dost thou not know one *Huluerhead*, that keepes
An Innocent in his house
Phi. There are few Innocents in the County S^r.
They are giuen too much to Law for that.
I doe not know him S^r.
Qui How knewst thou that I want a Servant?
Phi. Euen at an old wiues house S^r by *Bow-Lane*
That placeth Servants; where the mayd came in
That yo^u put out to day.

112. folke] forlke *MS*.

121. *Layons Inne*] Lyons Inn, an Inn of Chancery in the Inner Temple (Sugden).

122. Aunt] also, whore or bawd; "an *aunt*, like a *cousin*, is a very convenient relation" (Partridge).

122. *Muggle Street*] London street running south from St. Giles Cripplegate to Silver Street, and on which almshouses had been erected during the reign of Edward VI (Sugden).

125. *Thripperstowne*] a village near Norwich, the principal city of Norfolk (Sugden). Norfolk supported a cottage spinning industry, and the area was well known for worsteds (Ashley, *Life in Stuart England*, 12).

126. Rocks] distaffs used in spinning.

127. Thripping] spinning.

127. the] they; the omission of *y* may be an error, but it appears to reflect Phillis's adopted dialect.

130–31. The people of Norfolk "were credited with special love for lawsuits and skill in legal chicanery" (Sugden).

134. *Bow-Lane*] London street running south through Cheapside (Sugden), where an employment agency of sorts may have been located. See also Brome, *The City Wit*, I.i.296–300: "desire Mistress Piccadell in Bow-Lane . . . to provide me an honest, handsome secret young man that can write and read written hand."

Qui. Ah—And what said shee?
Phi. Truly to speake the best & worst forsooth
Shee said her fault deseru'd her punishment
For letting of her Mistres run away
Qui. The newes goes current. I am glad o'that.
[*Phi.*] And that yo^{u} were a very strict hard man [15^{r}]
But very iust; and that a dog should haue
His due of yo^{u}, and it were but a halter.
Qui. Ha ha ha.
Ph. And such a Master would I serve to choose S^{r}.
Qui. This Innocent countrey Mother takes me.
Her lookes speake hollsomnes; and that old woman
(That *Bow lane* Purveyor) has fitted me
Wth serviceable flesh these dozen yeares.
I'll keepe her at the least this Gander-month
Whilst my faire Wife lyes in of her black face
And Virgine Vow, In hope shee's for my turne.
Lust, when it is restraind, the more twill burne.
Come in I'll talke wth yo^{u}.
Phi. Prosper now my plot
Hulke thou art twixt wind & water shot. *Ex^{t}*

Scœne ii Enter Lucy & Theophilus.

Lu. Indeed yo^{u} were vnkind to turne away
My Mayd (poore harmles Maid) whose innocent Mirth
Was the best cheare yor house afforded me
But I forgiue it in yo^{u}, though I blame
And wish that I could chide that hasty humor
Out of yor blood.

142. *Phi.*] *no speaker change MS.* 152. face] face. *MS.* 157. Hulke] Hold Hulke ("Hold" *deleted*) *MS.*

146. serve to choose] To "serve" sometimes meant to copulate, but perhaps the word reversal simply underscores Phillis's affected rustic speech; the reversal occurs in both texts.

151. Gander-month] the month after a wife's confinement for childbirth; here, the month of Millicent's vow.

154. "Fire that's closest kept burns most of all" (Tilley, F265).

157. Hulke] hulk, a large ship or the ruined body of an extremely old one; insulting when applied to a person, as here to Quicksands.

157. twixt wind & water shot] "To shoot between wind and water" (Tilley, W436); to hit properly, just above waterline on a ship. Phillis's act has worked thus far.

The. Insooth I am sorry sister,
And wish I could recouer her. Yet (by yor leaue)
I saw her bold & rude w'yee, yes; & heard her
Say shee foresaw that *Arthure* my sole Enemy
Should marry yo^{u}. I'll marry yo^{u} to death first. *Ent: Arnold*
How now *Arnold*?
Me thincks I read good newes vpon thy face.
Ar. The best, S^{r}, I can tell yo^{u}, is, The Iew
Of *Mark-Lane* yonder, that devouring *Quicksands*
Has lost his faire young wife
The. What! Is she dead?
Ar. Tis not soe well for him. For if shee were dead
He might thinck to ouertake her, though she were gone
To'the devill. But shee is run away, most roundly
run away, wch has set vp such a Laughter in the towne
Among the Gallants—
The. And doe yo^{u} laugh too?
Ar. Yes; & if yo^{u} doe not outlaugh all men that haue
heard on't the Ioyfull newes is too good for yo^{u}.
The. I am too mercifull, that I kill thee not
Is this yor ioyfull newes.
Ar. Hold, pray S^{r} hold.
The. Neuer while I haue power to lift a hand
Against thee villaine.
Lu. For-beare good Brother.
The. Sister forbeare me
This is a cause turnes patience into fury.
Lu. *Arnold* forbeare his sight
The. And my house too
Ar. S^{r} I am gone *Ex^{t}*
The. Or villaine looke to dye, as oft as I shall see.
Lu. O brother y'are to passionate.
The That mischieuous old villaine sure has killd her
And now to hide his fact has hir'd this slaue
To lay a scandall on her for a Tombe-stone

38. oft] of *MS*.

16. *Mark-Lane*] London street running from Fenchurch Street south to Great Tower Street (Sugden); "To walk penniless in Mark Lane" (Tilley, M678); pun on "mark" as money.

I'll write her Epitaph my selfe wthin the heart
Of that vile Monster. Sister let me goe [15^{v}]
I'll find her in his bowells Ex^{t}.

Lu. I must not leaue yo^{u} soe *Ex^{t}.*

Scœne iii Enter. Drawer. Nathaniell. Vincent. Edmond. Buzzard.

Dra. Y'are wellcome gentlemen.
Nat. Let's haue good wine boy; That must be o^{r} wellcome
Dra. Yo^{u} shall. yo^{u} shall S^{r}.
Wthin. *Ambrose Ambrose*
Dra. Here here, Anon anon. I come I come *Ex^{t}*
Wthin *Ierome Ierome* draw a quart of the best Canary
Into the *Apollo*—
Buz. This is a Language, that I haue not heard
Yo^{u} vnderstand it Gentlemen
Vin. Soe shall yo^{u} anon m^{r} *Buzzard.*
Buz. Yo^{r} frend & *Ionathan Buzzard* kind Gentlemen
Nat. Excellent luck had we to meet wth thee frend *Buzzard*!
Iust as thy master cast thee off.
Buz. Iust S^{r}, as I was going I know not whither; and now
I am arriu'd at iust I know not where.
Tis a rich roome this! Ist not Goldsmiths hall?
Nat. It is a Tauerne, man, & here comes the wine. *Ent Drawere*
Fill boy—Here's to thee frend, a hearty draught *wth wine*
To cheare thee—What dost thou sigh? There
Off wth it man, Hang sorrow. Cheare thy heart—.
Buz. And truly, tis the best cheare I haue tasted.
Vin. Come tast it better. Heres another to thee.—
Buz. And truly this was better then the first.
Ed. Then try a third. That may be best of all.—
Buz. And truly soe it is. How many sorts of wine
May a Vintner bring in one pot togither?
Nat. By *Bacchus*, master *Buzzard*, that's a subtle question.
Buz. *Bacchus*! Who's that I pray.
Vin. A great frend of the Vintners; master of theyr

1–6. Cf. Shakespeare, *I Henry IV*, II.iv.

8. *Apollo*] the room of the Devil Tavern where Jonson's Tavern Academy met (Sugden).

17. Goldsmiths hall] the hall on the east side of Foster Lane that served as a meeting place for the Company of Goldsmiths (Sugden); it may have been opulent.

Company indeed.
Buz. I was neuer, in all my Life, soe farre in a Tauerne
before. What comforts haue I lost!
Ed. Now he beginnes to talke
Buz. Nor euer was, in all my fiue & twentie yeares
Capiuity, vnder that Tirant, that turnd me away,
Soe farre as a Vintners barre but thrice.
Nat But thrice in all that time
Buz. Truly but thrice S^{r}. And the first time was
To fetch a Gill of Sack for my Master & a frend
of his that ioynd wth him in a purchace of sixteene
thousand pound.
Vin. I marry! There was thrift. More wine boy.
Nat. A pottle & a beere bowle.
Buz. The second time was for a penny-pot of Muscadine
W^{ch} he himselfe dranke wth an egge vpon his
Wedding morning.
Nat. And to much purpose (it seemd) by his wiues running away.
Buz. The third & last time was for halfe a pint of Sack
Vpon his wedding night; when Hell broke loose
And all the devills daunc'd at our house: w^{ch}
Made my Master mad; whose raving made my
Mistres run away; whose running away was the [16^{r}]
Cause of my turning away. O me, poor masterles
Wretch that I am. o------o------
Nat. Hang thy Master. Here's a health to his confusion.
Buz. I thanck yo^{u}. Let it come S^{r}. ha ha ha.
Vin. Thinck noe more of Masters. Frends are better then Masters.
Buz. And yo^{u} are all my frends kind Gentlemen.
O how I loue kind Gentlemen.
Nat. That shewes thou art of gentle blood thy selfe frend *Buzzard*

38. *Nat*] *M. Nat* (*"M." deleted*) *MS.*

37. Vintners barre] the counter at the front of a tavern, or in an inn or other place of business, where liquor was sold.

40. Gill] one fourth of a pint, a small amount for such an occasion.

44. pottle] a half-gallon, usually of wine.

44. beere bowle] the vessel in which beer was served; a large drinking glass, normally used for beer.

45. penny-pot] one of the smallest of the wooden or pewter pots of alcohol sold for standard rates.

46. wth an egge] Wine with egg was sometimes believed to be an aphrodisiac.

49. halfe a pint] "An Usurers gallon, that's just halfe a pint" is traditional (Celeste T. Wright, "Some Conventions Regarding the Usurer in Elizabethan Literature," 186).

Buz. Yes Frend. Shall I call yo^{u} frend?
Ed Vin. By all meanes all of vs.
Buz. Why then all Frends; I am a Gentleman borne,
Though spoild in the breeding. The *Buzzards* are
all Gentlemen. We came in wth the conquerour
Our name (as the french has it) is *Beau-desert.*
W^{ch} signifies—Frends, what dos it singnify?
Vin. It signifies that yo^{u} deseru'd fairly of yor Master
When he turn'd yo^{u} away. And now here's a health
to him that first finds his wife, and sends
her home wth a bouncing boy in her belly for
him to father.
Buz. I'll pledge that. And then I'll tell yo^{u} a secret
Nat. Well said frend. Vp wth that. And then out wth thy secret.
Buz. This was an excellent draught. /hickvp/
Nat. But the Secret, frend; Out wth that
Buz. It might proue a shrewd matter against my Mischieuous
Master as it may be handled.
Nat Hang him cullion that would turne thee away.
Buz. Heark yee then all frends.—Shall I out wth it?
Vin. Yes by all meanes
Buz. Then I'll take tother cup; and out wth it all togither—hickvp.
Now catch, it comes ifaith. If my Mistres should bring my
Master home a bastard, she were but euen wth him.
Nat. He has on I warrant. ha! has he Cadzookes?
Buz. That he has by this most delicate drinck—But
It is the ougliest Arsivarsiest Aufe that euer came
the wrong way into the world. Sure some Goblin
got it for him; or chang'd it in the neast, that's certaine.
Nat. I vow thou vtterst braue things. Ist a boy?
Buz. It has gone for a boy in short coats, & long Coates

71. his] his wth ("wth" *deleted*) *MS*.

64–65. I . . . breeding.] "Birth is much but breeding is more" (Tilley, B402).

66. We came in wth the conquerour] pun on buzzards as seekers of spoil. Buzzard often has been compared with Jonson's Sir Amorous La-Foole, who similarly traces his pedigree in *Epicoene*.

78. shrewd] cunning and injurious.

80. cullion] vile and despicable rascal.

87. delicate] excellent.

88. Arsivarsiest] from "arsy-versey," or "arse" first; "contrary, perverse, preposterous" (*OED*).

88. Aufe] oaf.

These seauen & twenty yeares.
Ed. An Ideot is it?
Buz. A very Natrall; and lookes as old as I doe. And I
thinck if my beard were of I could be like him.
I haue taken great paines to practise his speech
and action to make myselfe merry wth him in the Countrey.
Nat. Where is he kept
Buz. In the further side of *Nor-folke*: where yo^{u} must
neuer see him. Tis now a dozen yeares since his
Father saw him. And then he compounded for a somme
of money wth an old man to keepe him for his life time:
And he neuer to heare more of him. But I saw him
Wthin these 3 monthes. We hearken after him as landsick
heires doe after their fathers in hope to heare of his end
at last.
Vin. But hearke yo^{u} frend. If yor beard were off, could yo^{u} be [16^{v}]
Like him thinck yo^{u}? What if yo^{u} cut it off; and to him
for a Father?
Buz. My beard? noe frend my beard's my honor.
Haire is an ornament of honor vpon man or woman.
Nat. *Mun*, knock him downe wth tother cup. Wee'll lay him
to sleepe; but yet watch & keepe him betwixt hawke &
Buzzard as he is, till we make excellent sport wth him.
Buz. *Heigh-hoe*—I am very sleepie.
Vin. See, he Iukes allready.
Nat. Boy, shew vs in to some lesse roome, that is more priuate.
Boy. This way S^{r}, and please yo^{u}. *Buzzard is lead off.*
Ex^{t} oes

119. SD *is*] *interlined with a caret MS.*

95. Natrall] half-witted from birth.

102. compounded] contracted.

112. Haire is an ornament of honor] Not only hair as "crowning glory": hair loss is one of the symptoms of the secondary stages of syphilis.

114–15. betwixt hawke & / Buzzard] literally, between the best (hawk) and worst (buzzard) of a species; confused and undecided, or in context here, probably tipsy and malleable; Tilley, H223.

117. Iukes] jukes, begins to sleep.

Scœne iiii. Enter. Arnold solus.

Turnd out of dores? A dainty frantick humor
In a young Master. Good enough for me though:
Because tis proper to old Servingmen,
To be soe seru'd. What course now must I take?
I am too old to seeke out a new Master.
I will not beg: because I'll crosse the prouerbe
That runs vpon old Serving creatures. And
Stealing's a hanging matter. I haue noe mind to't.
Wit & Invention helpe me wth some shift
To helpe a cast off now at a dead lift.
Sweet Fortune heare my sute. **Ent Nath:*

Nat. The onely fellow that I wishd to haue found.
Why how now *Arnold*, at thy deuotions?

Ar. O s^{r}. I am turnd away; and out of Service

Nat. Has thy mad Master seru'd thee soe too *Arnold*?

Ar. Why who's seru'd soe besides S^{r}?

Nat. One that I
Meane to make thee aquainted wth; by whome
Thou shalt get Peeces *Arnold*, & the meanes
To peece thee to thy master againe.

Ar. O S^{r}. Where is that happy meanes?

Nat. Goe presently to th'Deuill tauerne *Arnold*
And ask for *Mun*, & *Vince*. And I'll come to yo^{u}.

Ar. You'll not be long?

Nat. Not passing halfe an houre.

Ar. Fortune I hope thou hast heard me to the purpose. *Ex^{t}.*

Nat. Sweet Mirth, thou art my Mistres: I could serue thee,
And shake the thought off of all womankind,
But that old wonts are hardly left. A Man
That's enterd in his Youth, and throughly salted
In documents of women, hardly leaues
While Reines or braines will last him. Tis my case.

2. dainty] fastidious or scrupulous, often overly so.

2. frantick] wildly angry; foolish.

7–8. prouerbe . . . creatures] "An old servingman a young beggar" (Tilley, S255).

11. dead lift] desperate situation.

12. The SD in *O* reads: "*He kneels.*"

20. Peeces] money.

23. Deuill tauerne] Devil Tavern, frequented by Jonson.

33. Reines] kidneys (see note, III.i.68); the area of the kidneys, the loins.

Yet Mirth (when women faile) brings sweet incounters,
That tickle vp a Man aboue their Sphere;
They dull, but Mirth reviues a Man. Who's here? *Ent: Arthure*
The solitary musing man, calld *Arthure*,
Possest wth Serious Vanity; Mirth to mee.
The world is full. I cannot peepe my head forth
But I meet mirth in euery Corner still.
Sure some old Runt wth a splay foot hath crost him.
Hold vp thy head man. What dost seeke? Thy graue?
I would scarce trust yo^{u} wth a peece of earth
Yo^{u} would choose to lie in though; were some deft Lasse [17^{r}]
Or some plump Mistres set before yor search.
Ar. How vainly this man talkes.
Nat. Gid yee good den forsooth.
How vainly this man talkes! Speake but truth now
(For all yor sincere simprings to yor frend)
Dos not thy thoughts now run vpon a wench?
I neuer look'd soe but mine stood that way.
Ar. Tis all yor glory, that; and to make boast
Of the varietie that serues yor Lust:
Yet, not to know what woman yo^{u} loue best.
Nat. Not I (cadzookes) but all alike to mee,
Since I put off my [Wench] I kept at Liuorie.
But of their vse I thinck I haue had my share
And haue lou'd euery one best of living women.
A dead one I nere coueted, that's my comfort.
But of all Ages, that are pressable
From Sixteene vnto Sixty; and of all complections
From the white flaxen to the Tawney-Moore;
And of all Statures betweene dwarfe & Giantesse;

47. yee] yee d ("d" *deleted*) *MS*. 56. my [Wench] I] my I *MS*; my Wench I *O*.
62. the white] the wit white ("wit" *deleted*) *MS*.

41. Runt] "old woman, esp. an ill-favoured or ill-conditioned one"; this is the earliest appearance cited in the *OED*.

47. Gid yee good den] clipped form of "God give you good even," a salutation.

55–69. Cf. Donne, "The Indifferent."

56. my . . . Liuorie] i.e., Phillis.

62. flaxen] blond.

Of all Conditions from the doxie to the Dowsabell;
Of all Opinions (I will not say Religions:
For what make they wth any?) And of all
Features & shapes from the huckle-backd Bum-creeper,
To the streight spiny Shop-Mayd in St *Martins*;
Briefly all sorts & Sizes I haue tasted.
Ar. And thinckst thou hast done well in it.
Nat. As well as I could wth the worst of'em though I say't.
Few men come after me, that mend my worke.
Ar Thou dost not thinck of punishments to come:
Thou dream'st not of Diseases, Pouertie,
The Losse of Sense, or Member; or (the Crosse,
Common to such loose Livers) an ill Marriage,
A hell on earth to scourge thy Conscience.
Nat. Yes: when I marry, let me haue a wife
To haue noe mercy on mee. Let the fate
Of a stale doating batchelor fall vpon me.
Let me haue *Quicksands* curse, to take a wife
Will run away next day; and prostitute
Her selfe to all the world before her husband.
Ar. Nay that will be too good. If I foresee
Any thing in thy Mariage destiny:
Twill be to take a thing, that has bene common
To the world before; and liue wth thee perforce
To thy perpetuall torment.
Nat. Close that point.
I cannot marry. Will you be merry *Arthure*?
I haue such things to tell thee.
Ar. Noe: I cannot.
Nat. Pray thee come closer to me. What has crost thee?
Is thy suppos'd slaine Father come againe?

64. doxie] cant term for a vagabond's mistress; a prostitute.

64. Dowsabell] a sweetheart, or gentle lass.

67. huckle-backd] hump-backed.

67. Bum-creeper] "one who walks bent almost double" (*OED*).

68. St *Martins*] a section of London near the church of St. Martin-Le-Grand, which, because it retained right of sanctuary, was frequented by criminals and was so well known for its second-rate shops that cheap copper lace was called "St. Martin's lace" (Sugden).

80. stale] sexually unexciting; "stale" also meant "whore," so a "stale-doating" man might mean one foolish enough to dote on a whore.

To dispossesse thee for another life time?
Or has thy valiant Sister beaten thee?
Ar. Let yor valiant witt & iocound humor be suppos'd
Noe warrant for yo^{u} to abuse yor frends by.
Nat. Why didst tell me of marrying then.
But I haue done. And pray thee tell me now
What is the matter? What is it that grieues thee? [17^{v}]
Pray tell me.
Ar. Then I care not if I doe:
For twill be Towne-talke shortly.
Nat. Out wth it then.
Ar. My Sister—O *Nathaniell*, doe not mock
My griefe.
Nat. Yo^{u} see I doe not. What of her I pray?
Ar. My Sister on a priuate discontent
Betwixt herselfe & me hath left my house.
Nat. Gone quite away?
Ar. Yes; And I know not whither.
Nat. Beyond Sea sure, to fight wth th'Ayre that tooke
Her fathers last breath into't. Went shee alone?
Ar. Noe, noe. my Man's gone wth her.
Nat. Who the fellow
That braggs on's back soe? The stiffe strong-chin'd Rascall?
Ar. Euen he.
Nat. The devill is in these young Titts
And wildfire i'their Cruppers.
Ar. Let me charme yo^{u}
By all o^{r} Frendship, yo^{u} nor speake, nor heare
An ill construction of her act in this.
I know her thoughts are noble; and my woe
Is swolne vnto that fullnes, that the addition
But of a word, in scorne, would blow me vp
Into a Clowd of wild distemperd fury
Ouer the heads of such whose looser breath
Dare raise a wind to breake me. Then I fall
A sodaine Storme of Ruine on yo^{u} all. *Ex^{t}.*

97. valiant] worthy, excellent.
117. back] strength; sexual prowess.
119. Titts] also, hussies.
120. Cruppers] crupper, "leathern strap buckled to the back of the saddle and passing under the horse's tail" (*OED*); pudenda.
121. charme] entreat.

Nat. I know not how to laugh at this: It comes
Soe neare my pitty. But I'll to my Griggs
Againe; And there wee'll find new Mirth, to stretch
And laugh, like tickled wenches, hand ore head. *Ex^{t}.*

Scœne. v. Enter Dionisia in mans apparraile. *Rafe.*

Dio. How dos my habit, & my armes become me.
Ra. To well to be a woman, manly Mistres.
Soe well that I beginne to thinck yo^{u} are
A man indeed. Would yo^{u} would giue me leaue
To try alitle though.
Dio. How thinck yo^{u} now. *(Beats him*
Ra: Hold hold, heroick M^{r}is.
Soe many of these tryalls haue past vpon me
That all my flesh is beaten into brawne.
And my head codled. Yet whether the deuill, or what
Is in't I know not, I loue her still the more.
Her blowes kindle desire in me. They are my ticklings.
Dio. If I had not this fellow to beat sometimes
My fury would dye in me. But what's this
To th'Enemy of my blood? I must not rest
Till I strike there. Ha'yo^{u} got me a Pistoll.
Ra. Yes: here tis, & a good one
Dio. It is too long me thincks.
Ra. Noe Lady would wish a shorter. It would beare
Noe chardge, nor carry nothing home else Mistres.
Dio. I'll try what it can doe. Thou thinckst I am valiant
Ra. All the Viragos that are found in story
Penthesilea and *Symiramis* [18^{r}]

Scene v

20. beare] beare noe char ("noe char" *deleted*) *MS.*

132. Griggs] grig, "an extravagantly lively person, one who is full of frolic and jest" (*OED*); i.e., Edmond and Vincent.

Scene v

10. brawne] calloused skin.

11. codled] made soft; from "coddling," boiling or stewing fruits and vegetables.

17. Pistoll] also, as Rafe uses it, penis.

24. *Penthesilea*] the mythological Amazonian queen who fought for Troy and who was slain and mourned by Achilles.

24. *Symiramis*] Semiramis, the legendary warrior queen believed to have built Babylon. In Jonson's *Epicoene* (III.iv.57), Morose cries: "I have married a Penthesilea, a Semiramis."

Were noe such handy strikers as yo^{r}selfe.
But they had another stroke, could yo^{u} but find it;
Then yo^{u} were excellent. I could teach it yo^{u}.
Dio. As yo^{u} respect my honor or yor Life
See yo^{u} continue constant to my trust;
And be assur'd (allthough I promise nothing)
Thou canst not know how much I loue thee.
Ra. There is a hope as good now as a promise
Dio. Here, at this Inne abide, & wait my coming.
Be carefull of my gueldings. Be not seene
·Abroad for feare my brother may surprise yo^{u}.
There's money for yo^{u}; and ere that be spent
Tis like I shall returne. *Ex^{t}.*
Ra: Best starres attend yo^{u}.
Mars arme thee all the day, and *Venus* light
Thee home into these amorous armes at night. *Ex^{t}.*

Finis Actus tertii.

Act iiii. Scœne i.

Quicksands. Millicent. like a black Moore.

Qui. Be cheard my Loue. Helpe to beare vp the Ioy
That I conceaue in thy concealed beauty,
Thy rich imprison'd beauty, whose infranchisement
Is now at hand: When those illustrious Emblemes,
That Red & White, those two vnited houses,
(Whence Beauty takes her faire name & decent,)

30. nothing)] nothing *MS.* 31. Thou] Though *MS*; thou *O.* 32. *Ra.*] *Ra. Dio* ("*Dio*" *deleted*) *MS.*

25. strikers] persons who easily resort to blows; fornicators (the meaning Rafe plays on in lines 26–27).

34. gueldings] geldings.

Act iiii. Scene i

7. Red & White, those two vnited houses] red and white coloration, the ideal of feminine beauty; red and white roses, emblems of the houses of Lancaster and York.

8. A compliment that would have been more appropriate during the reign of Elizabeth, though not inappropriate in Caroline England. Interestingly enough, both Seymour and his first wife, Arabella Stuart, were considered claimants to the throne; James had forbidden their marriage, and he imprisoned them after it took place. The compliment occurs in both texts, however (III.i in *O*), and it probably was not in-

Shall (like my Gold and Iewells) be drawne againe
Out of their Ebon Casket, and shine forth
In their admired glory. I am rapt
Aboue the Sphere of common Ioy & wonder
In the effects of this o^{r} queint complot
Mil. In the meane time (though yo^{u} take pleasure in it)
My name has dearely sufferd.
Qui. But thine honor
Shall, in the vindication of thy name,
When Envy & Detraction are struck dumbe,
Gaine an eternall Memory wth Vertue:
When the discountenanc'd Witts of all my Iierers
Shall hang their heads & fall like leaues in *Autumne.*
Now note my plot; the height of my Invention.
I haue allready giuen out to some,
That I haue certaine knowledge yo^{u} are dead,
And haue had priuate buriall in the Countrey;
At wch my shame, not griefe, forbad my presence:
Yet some way to make knowne vnto the world
A husbands duty, I resolue to make
A certaine kind of feast, wch shall advance
My Ioy, aboue the reach of spight, or chance.
Mil. May I pertake S^{r}, of yor rich conceyt?
Qui. To morrow night expires yor Limitted Month
Of vow'd virginity. It shall be such a night! [18^{v}]
In wch I meane thy Beauty shall breake forth
And dazell wth amazement, euen to death
Those my malicious enemies, that reioyc'd
In thy suppos'd escape & my vexation.
Mil. Shall they then be yor guests?
Qui. They shall my sweet.
I will invite'hem all to such a feast,
As shall fetch blushes from the boldest guest.
I haue the first course ready

9. Gold] Gold) *MS.* The parenthesis may provide a semantic signal, but it is omitted here because it is syntactically confusing.

cluded simply to flatter Seymour. (Alexander Brome paid a similar compliment to Henry Huntingdon in his elegy in *Lachrymae Musarum*, the collection of elegies that Richard Brome edited in 1649.)

20. Iierers] jeerers.

Mil. And if I
Faile in the second blame my huswifry. *(Knock.*
[*Qui.*] Away; somebody comes. I guesse of them *(Ex^{t} Mil.*
That haue Iier'd me, whome I must Iiere agen. *Ent. Nathaniell*
Gallants, y'are wellcome. I was sending for yee. *Edmond. Vincent.*
Nat. To giue vs that we come for I am perswaded.
Qui. What may that be?
Vin. Trifles yo^{u} haue of ours.
Qui. Of yo^{r}s my Masters?
Ed. Yes yo^{u} haue in Mortgage
Threeskore pound land of mine Inheritance.
Vin. And my Annuity of an hundred Marks.
Nat. And Iewells, Watches, Plate & Cloathes of mine
Pawnd for foure hundred pounds. Will yo^{u} restore all?
Qui. Yo^{u} know all these were forfeited long since.
Yet I'll come roundly to yo^{u} gentlemen.
Ha'yo^{u} brought my moneyes & the Interest?
Nat. Noe surely. But wee'll come as roundly to yo^{u},
As monylesse gentlemen can. Yo^{u} know
Good offices are ready money.
Qui. Right.
But haue yo^{u} offices to sell? or would yo^{u}
Deale for some Courtier, that has?
Vin. Noe s^{r}.
We meane to doe yo^{u} offices for yor Money.
Qui. As how I pray yo^{u}?
Nat. Marry S^{r}, as thus.
I'll helpe yo^{u} to a Man, that has a frend—
Vin. That knowes a Party, that can goe to the house—
Ed. Where a Gentleman dwelt, that knew a Scholler—
Nat. That was exceeding well acquainted wth a Trauello^{r}.
Vin. That made report of a great Magitian beyond the Seas
Ed. That was the likeliest man in all the world

45. *Qui.*] *no speaker change MS.*

44. huswifry] housewifery, domestic management.

58. come roundly] deal with someone favorably and fully.

62. offices] services rendered; government positions to be bought and sold. Brome often employs the sort of wordplay that follows.

Nat. To helpe you to your wife agen.
Qui. You are the merriest Mates, that ere I cop'd wth.
But, to be serious Gentlemen; I am satisfied
Concerning my lost wife. She has made euen
Wth me, & all the world.
Ed. What! Is she dead?
Qui. Dead, dead. And therefore, as Men vse to mourne
For kind & loving wiues; and call their frends,
(Their choycest frends) vnto a solemne banquet
Serv'd out wth sighes & sadnes; I doe purpose,
Because tis plaine she lou'd not me, to invite
You & yor like, that lou'd her & not me,
To see me in the pride of my reioycings.
You shall find entertainment worth yor Company;
And that let me intreat tomorow night.
Ed. Vin. You shall haue mine.
Nat. Cadzookes we came to Iiere thee; wee
Thought to haue vext thee, till we made thee stinck [19r]
Like a ranck Iew as thou art, wth tales & things
We had devisd vpon thy wife. But now—
To morrow night you say.
Qui. Yes gallants, faile not, as you wish to view
Yor Mortgages & Pawnes againe. Adieu. *Ext.*
Ed. The Rogue Iieres vs.
Vin. How glad the Rascall is
For his wiues death
Nat. An honest man could not haue had the Luck.
Ed. He has some further drift in't (could we guesse it)
Then a meere Meriment for his dead wiues riddance
Vin. Perhaps he has got a new wife, & intends
To make a funerall & a Mariage feast
In one to hedge in chardges.
Ed. Hee'll be hang'd rather then marry agen.
Nat. Twould be a rare addition to his Mirth
For vs to bring our antick in betwixt hem

83. & loving] & loving & loving *MS.* 108. *Ed.*] *M Ed.* ("*M*" *deleted*) *MS.*

79–80. She . . . world] i.e., has died. Cf. Shirley, *Cupid and Death* (1653): "Death quits all scores" (Tilley, D148).

88. pride] also, height or most glorious moment.

110. antick] representation or perform-

I meane his changeling bastard, if he should
Marry some Iealous hilding.
Vin. How ere wee'll grace his feast wth o^{r} p^{r}sentment
Nat. Where's the *Buzzard.*
Ed. We left him wth his Foster father *Arnold*
Busy at rehersall, practising theyr parts.
Nat. They shall be perfect by to morrow night
If not vnto o^{r} proffit, our delight. *Ex^{t} oẽs.*

Scœne. ii. Theophilus. Lucy. Page.

Lu. Brother be comforted
The. Let not the name
Or emptie sound of comfort mixe wth the ayre
That must invade these eares. They are not capable;
Or, if they be, they dare not, for themselues,
Giue the conveyance of a sillable
Into my heart that speakes not griefe & sorrow.
Lu. Be grieu'd then; I'll grieue wth yo^{u}. For each sigh
You wast, in vayne, for *Millicents* timeles death
I'll spend a teare for yor as fruictles sorrow.
The. That's most vnsutable. Yo^{u} are noe company
For me to grieue wth, and grieue for me.
Take the same cause wth me: Yo^{u} are noe frend
Or Sister else of mine: It is enough
To set the world a weeping
Lu. All but the stony part
The. Now yo^{u} are right. Her husband's of that part
And cannot weepe by Nature. But I'll find

111. his] his anti ("anti" *deleted*) *MS.*

Scene ii

15. enough] enough to set ("to set" *deleted*) *MS.*

ance, usually grotesque; here Buzzard and Arnold.

111. changeling] used loosely to mean any half-witted or "different" person; here refers to Buzzard's substitution for Quicksands's son.

112. hilding] worthless woman, jade.

Scene ii

10. timeles] untimely.

By Art, a way in Chymistry, to melt him.
But doe yo^{u} weepe indeed for *Milicent*?
Lu. Yes brother
The. All these teares?
Lu. All for yor Loue.
The. She was my Loue indeed; and was my wife,
But for the poore bare name of Mariage onely
Lu. But now shee's yo^{r}s foreuer: Yo^{u} enioy her
In her faire blessed Memory, in her Goodnes
In all that has prepar'd her way for glory. [19^{v}]
The. Let me embrace thee Sister. O how I reuerence
Any faire honor that is done to her.
Now thou shalt weepe noe more: Thou hast giuen me comfort
In shewing me how shee's mine.
And teares, indeed,
Are all too weake a Sacrifice for her
But such as the heart weepes.
Lu. Sit downe good Brother.
Sing boy, the mournefull song I bad yo^{u} practise.

Song.

Loue, where is now thy Deitie,
When *Fortune* alters thy decree;
In making of another blest
Wth her, thou plantedst in my brest?
And, *Fortune*, where is thy despight,
That gau'st another my delight;

20. Chymistry] Chymi ("y" *written over* "i"; "Chymi" *deleted*) Chymistry *MS*. 21. But] *Lu*. But ("*Lu.*" *deleted*) *MS*. 22. Yes] All for Yes ("All for" *deleted*) *MS*. 32. Now] T Now ("T" *deleted*) *MS*. 32. me comfort] me / comfort *MS*. "Comfort" is written below "giuen me" as a runover. 40–55. The entire song may have been meant to be set apart in italic hand, as were the song snatches of I.iii. This portion of the manuscript appears to have been written hurriedly, and several words contain more italic letters than usual. Since most words are in the normal mixed hand, however, I have reproduced the song in roman

20. In *O* a line has been added—"At least extract some drops"—which would clarify Theophilus's intentions.

40–55. The song is well-adapted to the situation of the play and is likely to have been written for *The English Moor*. It is not included in *O*, and, as far as I have been able to determine, is published for the first time here. (The song probably did not appear in the manuscript from which *O* was taken; such omissions were common. See William R. Bowden, *The English Dramatic Lyric*, 87–94, for a discussion of printing practices and the lost songs.)

44. despight] contempt or disdain for others.

When *Death* has tane from him & thee
The precious prize, as well as mee?

Of *Loue* I blame th'Inconstancie;
Of *Fortune* curse the Crueltie;
Death, my Reuenger, yet, shall scape
Though he has done the greatest Rape
    For he is kindest of the three
In taking her he calls for mee.
His kindnes carries yet a blot:
For though he calls he takes me not.

The. Call yo^{u} this mournefull? Tis a wanton Ayre.
Goe; y'are a naughty child; Indeed I'll whip yo^{u}
If yo^{u} giue voyce vnto such notes hereafter. *Ex^{t} Page.*
Lu. I know not brother how yo^{u} like the Ayre:
But in my mind the words are very sad
Pray read hem S^{r}. *He reades.*
The. I thanck yo^{u} Sister. They are sad indeed.
How now my boy? dost weepe? I am not angry. *Ent: Page. weeping.*
I haue forgiuen thee now.
Pa: I doe not weepe
S^{r} for my selfe. But there's a Youth wthout;
A handsome Youth, whose sorrow works in mee.
A sayes he wants a Service, and seekes yo^{rs}
The. Dost not know him.

---

type, with the names, which are primarily in italic hand, italicized. 56–64. In the manuscript, these lines are indented to correspond with the song; but from line 65 on, the speeches return to the normal left-hand margin. I have set only the song apart, as was the intention.

56. Tis a wanton Ayre] "Air" carried two meanings: (1) the melody of a song (see lines 59–60); and (2) a song less regular in form, but more sophisticated in lyrics and melody, than a ballad. On the basis of the first meaning, and Lucy's remarks (lines 59–60), R. W. Ingram has suggested that perhaps "sad words have been put to a well-known air used for a popular bawdy song or loose ballad, and an incongruous comic effect gained in this way" (Ingram, "The Musical Art of Richard Brome's Comedies," 233). This may well be true; but several lines would have been lost because of audience laughter, and songs such as this one were usually featured. It also seems possible that the music did suit the lyrics and that the comic incongruity derived from the contrast between the audience's sympathetic response to the song and Theophilus's "hasty" reaction. Lucy's comment, then, would be another example of the wordplay of which Brome was so fond.

Pa: Noe truly but I pitty him.
The. O good boy
That canst weepe for a strangers Misery
The sweetnes of thy deare compassion
Euen melts me too. What dos he say he is
Pa: Tis that S^{r} will grieue yo^{u}, when yo^{u} shall heare it.
Hee is a poore kinseman to the Gentlewoman
Lately deceasd, and yo^{u} soe truly mourne for
The. And dost thou let him stay wthout soe long?
Merciles villaine: Run & fetch him quickly
Lu O brother
The. Sister; can I be too zealous
In such a Cause, as this? For hearke yo^{u} Sister, *Ent. Page &.* [20^{r}]
Dio. There was noe way, like this, to get wthin'hem. *Dionisia*
Now, courage, keepe true touch wth me. I'll vexe
Yo^{r} cunning & vnnaturall purpose, brother;
If I doe nothing else.
Pa. S^{r}, here's the Youth.
The. A comely fac'd one tis; and wondrous like
That perfect marke of Vertue, my faire *Millicent.*
O let me run & clasp him; hang about him,
And yoake him to me wth a thousand kisses.
I shall be troublesome & heauy to thee
Wth the pleas'd weight of my incessant Loue,
Youth, of a happy kindred, wch fore-runs
A happy fortune euer. Pray thee Sister
Is he not very like her?
Lu. If I durst,
I would now say, This is the better beauty
For it resembles *Arthures.*
The. Why, Sister yo^{u} were wont to take delight
In any comfort that belong'd to me;
And helpe to carry my Ioyes sweetly. Now
Yo^{u} keepe noe constant course wth me.
Dio. This man melts me.
Alasse S^{r} I am a poore boy.

78. him] him him (*latter* "him" *deleted*) *MS.* 81. can] ca can ("ca" *deleted*) *MS.*
82. SD *Page &*] *interlined with a caret MS.*

The. What! and allyed to her? Impossible.
Disgrace not thy selfe soe, or her blood wthin thee.
Where ere thou liu'st her name's a fortune to thee;
Her memory, amongst good men, setts thee vp:
It is a word that commands all in this house.
Yet looke vpon him Sister. here; stand here.
Dio. This snare was not well laid: I feare my selfe.
The. Liue my companion, my especiall Sweet one.
My brother & my bedfellow thou shalt be.
Dio.. By Lakin but I must not: Though I find
But weake matter against it. Is this my courage!
The. Shee tooke from earth, how kind is Heauen, how good,
To send me yet a Ioy soe neare in blood?
Good, noble Youth, if there be any more
Distrest of yo^{u}, that claimes allyance wth her
(Though a farre off) deale freely; let me know it;
Giue me their sad names: I'll seeke them out;
And like a good great Man, in memory humble,
Not cease vntill I place them all in fortunes,
And see them grow about mee.
Dio. I heare of none, my selfe excepted S^{r}.
The. Thou shalt haue all my care then, all my Loue
Dio. What make I here? I shall vndoe my selfe.
The. Yet note him Sister. Here, now stand on this side
Dio. I there's the marke my Malice cheifely aymes at:
But then he stands soe neare I wound him too:
I feele that must not be: Art must be shewn here.
The. Come yo^{u} shall kisse him for me; and bid him wellcome.
Lu. Yo^{u} are most wellcome S^{r}. And were her name,
To wch yo^{u} are a kinseman, here a Stranger,
Vnheard of in this place, yet S^{r}, beleeue me,
In those faire eyes yo^{u} bring yor wellcome wth yo^{u}.
Dio. Neuer came Malice 'mong soe sweet a people:
It knowes not how to looke, nor I vpon them.
Lu. Let not yor gentle Modestie make yo^{u} seeme

115. By Lakin] contracted form of "By Our Lady."

123. in memory humble] i.e., a great man who remembers his humble beginnings or whose greatness has not affected his humility, so that he helps those less fortunate, instead of scorning them.

Vngentle to vs, by turning soe away.
The. That's well said Sister: But he will, & shall [20v]
Be bolder wth vs ere we part.
Dio. I shall: Too much I feare if my first resolution
Reuiue in me againe.
The. Come gentle blessing
Let not a Misery be thought on here,
If euer any were soe rude to touch thee.
Betweene vs wee'll devide the comfort of thee. *Ext oes.*

Scœne. iii. Enter. Millicent. & Phillis.

Mil. I haue heard thy story often; and wth pitty
As often thought vpont; and that the father
Of my best lou'd *Theophilus*, togither wth
His then frend mr *Meanewell* (who haue since
Become each others deathes-man, as tis thought)
By sutes in Law, wrought the sad ouerthrow
Of thy poore fathers fortune: By wch meanes
(Poore Gentleman) he was inforc'd to leaue
His natiue countrey to seeke forraine meanes
To maintaine Life.
Phil. Or rather to meet death.
For since that time, now six long twellmonths past
I neuer heard of him.
Mil. Much pittifull.
Phil. Soe is yor story, Mistres, vnto me:
You haue told, & I haue noted it wth teares.
But let vs dry our eyes, and know we must not
Stick in the mire of pitty, but wth labour
Worck or deliuery. Yors may be at hand,
If you set will & braine to't. But my honor
(If a poore wench may speake soe) is soe crackt
Wthin the Ring, as 'twill be hardly solderd
By any art. Fy on that wicked fellow,
That struck me into such a desperate hazard.
Mil. Hee will be here to night, & all the crew:

22–23. crackt / Wthin the Ring] "(of a coin) having the circle broken that surrounds the sovereign's head" (Onions): a coin so cracked could be refused as currency; loss of virginity.

And this must be the night of my deliuery
Out of this thralldome, I am prevented else
Foreuer Wench.
Phil. Why m^{rs}. can yo^{u} thinck
Our plot is not well cast
Mil. But we may faile
In the cariage of it. I, for my escape,
May put my selfe into the hands of one,
As dangerous to my honor, as this *Quicksands*
Is to my peace & Life. Yet I will venter
Peace, honor Life, all that I haue, or am
Wth a meere stranger, rather then trust my selfe
Vnder his roofe, that for his sinnefull lust
Would giue his faith to thee, his Soule to the deuill
And I aliue, & here.
Phil. But he told me that yo^{u} were dead; & I
Might liue to be his bride vpon the grant
Of a nights Lodging; he not dreaming I
Had made discouery of an English face
Vnder a *Barbary* dye, & his more base
And barbarous Vsage.
Mil. I'll be gone: That's certaine
Phil. Among the Guests, when they are come, make choyce
Of the most ciuill one to be yor convoy [21^{r}]
Be resolute & feareles.
Mil. Peace. He comes
Phil. I'll to my shift then. *Ex^{t}. Ent Quick-sands*
Qui. Where's my hidden Beauty?
That shall this night be glorious
Mil. I but wayt
The good houre S^{r}, for my deliuerance
Out of this base obscuritie
Qui. Tis at hand
Soe are my Guests. *See, some of them are enterd **Ent Nath Arthure.*
O my blith frend m^{r} *Nathaniell*, wellcome
And m^{r} *Arthure Meanewell*, as I take it.

44. dreaming] dreaning *MS.*

Nat. Yes S^{r}; a gentleman much sad of late
Whome I had much a doe to draw along
Yo^{u} say here shall be Mirth. How now! what's that?
Quic. That here shall gentlemen, I'll promise yo^{u}.
Nat. Ha'yo^{u} a black Coneybury in yor house?
Quic. Stay *Catelyna*. Nay shee may be seene
For knowe sirs I am mortified to beauty
Since my wiues death. I will not keepe a face
Better then this vnder my roofe, not I.
Yet I'll be merry too.
Art. Yo^{u} were too rash;
Too vnadvised in that willfull oath
Qui. Tis done & past S^{r}.
Nat. If I be not taken wth yond funerall face,
And her two eyes the Scutcheons, would I were whipt now
Art. Suppose yor frends should wish yo^{u} to a Match
Prosprous in wealth & honor
Qui. I'll heare of none
Art. Nay, I haue done.
Mil. That is a ciuill gentleman. But enemy
Vnto my best belou'd.
Nat The handsomst rogue
I haue euer seene yet, of a deed of darknes.
Tawny & russet faces I haue dealt wth:
But neuer came soe deepe in blacknes yet.
Qui. Come hither *Catelyna*. Yo^{u} shall see
What a braue wench shee shall be made anon.
And when shee daunces S^{r} yo^{u} shall admire her

74. rash;] rash; too vnadvised ("too vnadvised" *deleted*) *MS.*

67. Quicksands responds in abbreviated form to the statement Nat makes before he sees Millicent; "That" refers to "Mirth," as though Quicksands has said "Mirth here *shall* be, gentlemen." ("Here" may also be a slip for "there.")

68. Coneybury] a rabbit warren or burrow; slang for a loose woman.

69. *Catelyna*] the name Quicksands has given to the disguised Millicent.

77. funerall] pertaining to a funeral; dark.

78. Scutcheons] funeral escutcheons, the tablets exhibiting the heraldic emblems of deceased persons, attached to the front of monuments.

88. soe . . . yet] The black paint doubtless made the actor's face blacker than natural skin color.

Nat. He keepes this Rie Loafe for his owne white tooth
I'll haue a slyuer though I loose my whittle.
Qui. Here take this key; twill lead thee to those ornaments
That deckt thy Mistres lately: Vse her Casket;
And, wth the sparckling of her Iewells, shine;
Flame like a Midnight beacon, wth that face;
Or a pitcht ship on fire, the streamers glowing
And the keele mourning. Get thee glorious
Be like a running fire worke in my house
Nat. He sets me more a fire at her. Well old Stickbreech
If I doe chance to meet yor *Barbary* buttock
In all her brauery, and get a snatch
In an od Corner, or the darke to night,
(To mend yor cheare, & yo^{u} hereafter heare on't)
Say there are as good stomachs as yor owne.
Hist *Negro* hist.
Mil. Noe, fee, o noe I dare a not a.
Nat. Why, why, pish-pax I loue thee [21^{v}]
Mil. O noe the fine-a whit-a Gentillman-a
Cannotta loue-a the black-a thing-a.
Nat. Cadzookes the best of all wench.
Mil. O tacka heeda, my Mastra see-a.
Nat. When we are alone then, wilt thou?
Mil. Then I sall speak-a more-a. *Ex^{t}.*
Nat. And I'll not loose thee for more-a then I'll speak-a.
Qui. I muse the rest of my invited Gallants
Come not away. *Ent. Testy*

92. Rie Loafe] brown bread, and thus, Millicent as a dark woman; the reference is to sexual appetite.

92. Tooth] "To have a wanton tooth" (Tilley, T420).

93. slyuer] "It is safe taking a shive of a cut loaf" (Tilley, T34).

93. loose my whittle] whittle, a carving knife or small clasp-knife; penis. The phrase may allude to a popular association of Moors with sexual diseases (Elliot Harvey Tokson, "The Popular Image of the Black Man in English Drama, 1550–1688," 187).

98. pitcht ship] caulked with pitch, which would make it burn more quickly and brightly.

98. streamers] flags; flames shooting up like flags.

103. snatch] quick copulation.

106. stomachs] a reference to sexual appetite; the suggestion is that many would find such intercourse repugnant.

108. fee] probably "fay," a quasi-oath adding intensity, and a corruption of "By my faith."

109. pish-pax] "pish," a common exclamation; "pax," meaning "peace," or as a corruption of "pox."

118. Come not away] do not arrive.

Nat. Zookes, the old angry Iustice.
Tes. How comes it S^{r} to passe, that such a newes
Is spread about the towne? Is my Neece dead,
And yo^{u} prepar'd to mirth sir, hah s^{r} hah?
Is this the entertainment I must find
To wellcome me to towne?
Qui. You'll find content anon.
I'll instantly provide that cheare & Musique
Shall crowne yor wellcome wth delight & comfort
She is not dead S^{r}: but take yo^{u} noe notice *(whisper)*
Let me intreat yo^{u} S^{r}, to take the power
Of Master of this house among my Guests
Whilst I wthin prepare an Entertainment
To fill yo^{u} all wth wonder. *Ex^{t}*
Tes. Sure he is mad.
Or doe yo^{u} vnderstand his meaning Sirs?
Or how, or where his wife dyed?
Nat. I know nothing.
But giue me leaue to feare, by his wild humor
Hee's conscious of her death. Therefore I hope
Hee'll hang himselfe anon before vs all
To raise the Mirth he speakes of.
Art. Fy vpon thee.
Yet trust me S^{r}, there haue bene large constructions,
And strong presumptions, the ill made match, betwixt
Her youthfull beauty, & his couetous age,
Betwixt her Sweetnes & his frowardnes
Was the vnhappy meanes of her destruction.
Tes. Is it thought soe?
Art. Yes S^{r}: and (pardon me)
Yo^{r}selfe that gaue strength to that ill tyed knot
Doe suffer sharply in the worlds opinion,
While shee (sweet virgine) has it's generall pitty.
Tes. Pray what haue yo^{u} bene to her that haue spoke
Soe affectionatly of her? I nere found yo^{u}

143. presumptions,] presumptions, That ("That" *deleted*) *MS*; presumptions, that *O*.

140. raise the Mirth] amuse us; perhaps also a reference to the idea that hanging produces an erection.

Appeare a Suter to her.
Art. I neuer saw her
Nor euer should haue sought her S^{r}; for shee
Was onely Loue to my sworne Enemy;
On whome yet, were she living, in my guift,
Rather a thousand times I would bestow her
Then on that man that had but could not know her
Tes. I haue done ill; and wish I could redeeme
This act wth halfe my estate
Nat This devills bird
This Moore runs more & more still in my mind. *Ent. Vincent* [22^{r}]
O, are yo^{u} come? And haue yo^{u} brought yor Scene *Edmond.*
Of mirth along wyee?
Vin. Yes o^{r} Actors
Are here at hand. But we perceaue much busines
First to be set on foot; a shew of *Blackamores*
Nat. But saw yo^{u} not a Moore-hen there among hem
Ed. A pretty litle Rogue
Nat. Ah—
Vin. Most richly deckt
Nat. Ah—
Ed. Wth pearles, chaines, & Iewells. Shee's the queene
Of the nights triumph.
Nat. If yo^{u} chance to spy me
Take her aside, say nothing.
Vin. Thou wilt filch some of her Iewell perhaps
Nat. I'll draw a lot for the best Iewells she weares. *Ent: Quicksands.*
Qui. Enter the house pray Gentlemen. I am ready
Now wth yor Entertainment *Ex^{t}.*
Tes. Wee'll follow yo^{u}.
Nat. Now for six penny custards, a pipkin of bak'd peares
Three sawcers of stewd prunes, a groats worth of
Strong ale, & two pennyworth of Gingerbread. *Ex^{t}. Nat. Vinc. Edm.*
Tes. I like yor conversation S^{r}, soe well

155. I] Nor euer I ("Nor euer" *deleted*) *MS.*

182. Entertainment] Entertainnent *MS.*

163. devills bird] bird (also, woman) of the devil, black and possibly wicked.

184. pipkin] small earthenware dish. Nat expects pitiful fare, not a feast.

That let me tell yo^{u} briefly, if she liue
(As he beares me in hand she is not dead)
If all the Law bodily & Ghostly,
And all the Conscience too, that I can purchace
Wth all the wealth I haue, can take her from him
I will recouer her; and then bestow her
(If yo^{u} refuse her) on yor foe yo^{u} speake of
(Whose Right shee is indeed) rather then he
Shall hold her longer. Now mine eyes are opend.
Will yo^{u} walke in?
Art. I pray excuse me S^{r}.
I cannot fit my selfe to mirth.
Tes. Yo^{r} pleasure *Ex^{t}. Ent. Millicent*
Mil. Haue I wth patience wayted for this houre *White, as at*
And dos feare check me now? I'll breake through all *first.*
And trust my peace wth yond meeke Gentleman.
He cannot but be noble.
Art. A goodly creature
The roome's illuminated wth her; yet her looke
Sad, & cheeke pale, as if a Sorrow suckd it.
How came shee in? What is shee? I am feare-struck.
Tis some vnresting shadow—or, if not,
What makes a thing soe glorious in this house,
The Master being an Enemy to beauty?
She modestly makes to me.
Mil. Noble S^{r}.
Art. Speakes too!
Mil. If euer yo^{u} durst owne a goodnes,
Now crowne it by an act of honor & mercy.
Art. Speake quickly, loose noe time then: Say, what are yo^{u}?
Yo^{u} looke like one that should not be delayd.
Mil. I am th'vnfortunate woman of this house;
To all mens thoughts at rest. This is the face,
On wch the Hell of Iealousie abus'd

218. delayd] deny'd delayd ("deny'd" *deleted*) *MS.*

190. bodily] temporal.
190. Ghostly] spiritual, divine; Church law.
203. meeke] kind, courteous.
209. shadow] ghost of the dead.
212. makes to] comes toward.

The hand of Heauen, to fright the world wthall.
Art. Were yo^{u} the seeming Moore, was here?
Mil. The same. [22^{v}]
And onely to yor secresie & pitty
I haue venterd to appeare my selfe againe.
Art. Not to be lost in any thing concernes
My duty to yor peace, pray speake, wch way
Will yo^{u} command me? See if I be slothfull.
What's to be done? Pray speake & tis perform'd
Mil. In trust & Manhood, S^{r}, I would com̃it
A great chardge to you; euen my Life & honor,
To free me from this denne of Miserie.
Art. A blessed tasque! But when yo^{u} are free'd, Lady,—
Mil. I would desire S^{r}, then, to be conveyd—
Art. Whither? to whome? Speake quickly
Mil. Pray let that rest. I will releeue yor trouble
When I am freed from hence, & vse some others
Art. Nay, that were crueltie. As yo^{u} loue Goodnes tell me.
Mil. Why dare yo^{u} beare me S^{r}, to one yo^{u} hate?
Art. What's that, if yo^{u} loue? Tis yor peace I waite on;
I looke vpon yor Service, not mine owne.
Were he the mortallst Enemy flesh bred vp,
To yo^{u} I must be noble.
Mil. Yo^{u} professe most fairly.
Art. By all that's good & gracious I will dy
Ere I forsake yo^{u} till I set yo^{u} safe
Wthin those walls you seeke.
Mil. Then as we passe I'll tell yo^{u} where they stand s^{r}.
Art. Yo^{u} shall grace me. *Ex^{t}.*

Scœne iiii. Quicksands. Testy Nathaniell. Vincent. Edmond.

Qui. Now to o^{r} Reuells. Sitt yee, sit yee Gallants.
Whilst, Vncle, yo^{u} shall see how I'll requite
The Masque they lent me on my wedding night.
(Twas but lent Gentlemen,) yor Masque of hornes,
Wth all the private Iieres & publique scornes
Yo^{u} haue cast vpon me since. Now shall yo^{u} see
How I'll restore them, & re-married be
Vin. To anger vs, I hope hee'll marry his Moore.

Nat. I'll giue him something wth her, if I catch her
And be but in the Colehouse.

A florish

Tes. Attend Gentlemen.

Ent: Actor like a Moore leading in Phillis, black, & brauely deckt.

Actor. The queene of *Ethiope* dreampt vpon a night
Her black wombe should bring forth a virgine white

Ed. Black wombe

Actor. She told her King, he told thereof his Peeres
Till this white dreame filld their black heads wth feares.

Nat. Ah whoreson Blockheads.

Actor. Black heads I sayd. I'll come to you anon.
Till this white dreame filld their black heads wth feares.
For tis noe better then a Prodigee
To haue white Children in a black Contree.
Soe twas decreed, that if the Child prou'd white
It should be made away. O cruell spight
The queene cry'd out

Nat. Tis suppos'd shee was wth child then.

Actor. I'll be wth you anon Gentlemen.
The queene cry'd out, and was deliuered
Of child black, as you see: yet wizards said
That, if this damsell liu'd to married be
To a white Man, shee should be white as hee. [23r]

Ed. The Morrall is, if *Quicksands* marry her,
Her face shall be as white as his conscience.

Act. The carefull queene conclusion for to try
Sent her to merry *England* charily
The fairest Nation Man yet euer saw
To take a husband, such as I shall draw

11. Colehouse] coal house; "cole," however, was a slang term for money, so the reference could be to something like "accounting office"; perhaps also a pun on sexual relations with a black woman.

14. The story of Theagenes and Chariclea, the adventures of the white daughter of the black Ethiopian queen, from Heliodorus's *Æthiopica*, probably was familiar to Caroline audiences. See Joseph Quincy Adams, "Hill's List of Early Plays in Manuscript," 80–81; and Bentley, *Jacobean and Caroline Stage* 3:269.

19. whoreson] bastard son, a term of contempt; sometimes, as here, used jocularly.

35. conclusion] proposition or experiment.

37. fairest] most excellent; light-complected. Brome has drawn on his familiarity with Jonson's works for this masque: in *The Masque of Blackness* (1605), England is the glorious country where the sun can "blanch an ÆTHIOPE" (l. 255); and palmistry is central to *The Gipsies Metamorphosed* (1621). "To wash an Ethiop white" is proverbial (Tilley, E186).

Being an *Egiptian* Prophet.
Ed. Draw me, & I'll hang thee.
Act. Now I come to yo^{u} Gentlemen.
Qui. Now marke my Iieres.
Act. Yo^{u} must not haue her for I find by yor hand
Yo^{u} haue forfeited the Mortgage of yor Land.
Ed. Pox o'yor Palmestrie.
Vin. Now me.
Act. Nor yo^{u}: For here I plainely see
Yo^{u} haue sold & spent yor Liues Annuity.
Vin. The deuill take him that made thee a Soothsayer.
Nat. I find from whence yor skill comes: yet take me
For thy litle Princesse of Darknes; & if
I rub her not as white as another can,
Let me be hang'd vp wth her, for a new
Signe of the Labour in Vaine.
Act. Noe Sir.
The onely sute yo^{u} weare smells of the chest
That holds in Limbo-Lauender all yor rest.
Nat. I would his braines were in thy belly, that keepes the key on't
Act. This is the worthy man whose wealth & wit,
To make a white one must the black marke hit.
Qui. Yo^{r} Iieres are answerd Gallants. Now yor daunce
Enter 6. Blackamores. Daunce. *Ex^{t} Actor, & the rest of Moores.*
Nat. I hope you'll giue me leaue S^{r}, to take forth
Yo^{r} black brid, here, in a daunce
Qui. Wth all my heart S^{r}.

40. Draw] perhaps also a pun on "draw," as in pulling a man's penis from his clothing as one would pull a sword from a scabbard (Partridge).

54. Labour in Vaine] The image may be of a shop sign, but "You labor in vain to wash an Ethiop white" is proverbial and appears in a variety of forms throughout the Renaissance. In John Fletcher's *Knight of Malta*, Zanthia, a black maid, is called "My little labor in vain" (Eldred D. Jones, *The Elizabethan Image of Africa*, 48). The phrase may have had other implications, too. A ballad entitled "Labour in vaine" was entered in the Stationers' Register to Thomas Lambert on 18 June 1636 (Edward Arber, ed., *A Transcript of the Registers of the Company of Stationers of London, 1554–1640* A.D. 4:340). The ballad deals with "the torment that Lovers endure" and is reprinted in *The Roxburghe Ballads*, ed. William Chappell, 1:592–95.

57. Limbo-Lauender] pawn lavender; lavender was used to protect stored clothes from moths.

65. brid] bride; bird. *O* reads "bride," which certainly suits the context of the masque, but given the nature of Nat's interest in the Moor, "bird" is also a possibility.

Nat. Yo^{u} know what yo^{u} promisd me *Bullis*. Play a Galliard Musique.
Phil. But Howa can itta be done-a.
Nat. How I am taken wth the elevation of her Nosthrills!
Play alitle quicker. Hearke yo^{u}. If I lead yo^{u}
A daunce to a Couch, or a bedside yo^{u}'ll follow me
Phil. I will doe a my a besta.
Nat. And if I make thee not my beasta; & play not the
Beast wth thee too cut my Codpeece point. *(He daunces*
Soe soe. quick Musique quick *vily.*
Qui. O ougly! Call yo^{u} this dauncing ha ha ha—
Nat. Doe you laugh at me *He daunces her quite away & sodainly*
Arn. By yor leaue Gentlefolkes *Enter Arnold like an old countrey man*
Buz. O braue o braue o braue. *And Buzzard like a Changling. the*
Qui. How now! *Musick continuing.*
Tes. What are these?
Buz. Hark yee there. hack yee there. hack yee there:
O braue! Hey toodle loodle loodle loodle looe. *he daunces. &c.*
Qui. What are yee. Men or deuills?
Arn. Yo^{u} are advisd enough S^{r} and yo^{u} please.
But to be short I'll shew yo^{u}. I am a *Norfolke* man S^{r}.
And my name is *Iohn Huluerhead.*
Qui. Hold thy peace.
Ar. You can not heare o'that side then ta seemes.

73. thee] thy *MS.* 78. SD *sodainly*] *runs off the page MS.* 80. SD *man*] *runs off the page MS.* 90. *Huluerhead.*] *Huluerhead.* (*Qui* / Hold thy peace. *MS.* In this text, "*Qui.* Hold thy peace." appears on line 91 in standard format, as was the intention. 92. *Ar.*] *Ar Qui.* ("*Qui*" *deleted*) *MS.*

67. *Bullis*] bullace, a wild black plum; figurative term for sparkling black eyes. R. W. Ingram has suggested that "*Bullis*" refers to John Bull, a famed organist, who wrote galliards (Ingram, "The Musical Art of Richard Brome's Comedies," 232); but as we have no evidence that Nat had made arrangements with the musicians—"Yo^{u} know what yo^{u} promisd me"—and we *have* heard Nat's conversation with the disguised Millicent, it is reasonable to assume that the line is directed to the disguised Phillis.

67. Galliard] a lively, triple-time dance.

73–74. play not the / Beast] to "play the beast" is to engage in intercourse.

85. hack] indeterminate: possibly (1) *hack*, the chopping motion associated with a rock and spindle (see SD, lines 102–4); or (2) *hake*, idly running hither and yon (dialect). The first meaning seems the more probable. Perhaps he is "innocently" substituting "hack," with which the son would be very familiar, for the less-familiar "hark."

86. toodle loodle] the sound made by a person imitating a flute or pipes.

92. also, "He cannot hear on that side" (Tilley, E11), meaning he has heard what displeases him. (See line 99.)

Qui. I know thee not, not I.
Ar. But yo^{u} know my brother *Mathew Huluerhead*
Deceast, wth whome yo^{u} plac'd this child of yo^{r}s. Say yo^{u}. [23^{v}]
Qui. I say thou knowst not what thou sayst. I plac'd noe
Child in *Norfolke*, nor *Suffolk*, nor any folke I.
(Say thou mistookst me, and I'll reward thee. Goe.)
Ar. I cannot heare o'that eare naither S^{r}.
Vin. What's the matter m^{r} *Quicksands*?
Ed. Ha'yo^{u} any more Iieres to put vpon vs? What are those?
Buz. Hay toodle loodle loodle looe. *He spinnes*
Qui. O deuilish mischiefe. Get yo^{u} out of my house. *wth a rock*
Ar. I may not, till I be righted. I came for right *& spindle*
And I will haue right: or the best in the Citty
Shall heare on't.
Vin. Besworne the Rascalls act it handsomely
Tes. What art thou fellow? what dost thou seeke?
Vin. Yes, tell that gentleman. he is an vpright Magistrate
And will see thee righted.
Ar. I am a poore *Norfolk* man S^{r}. And I come to ease
me of a chardge that lies vpon my hands, by putting
Of a Child natrall to the natrall father here.
Qui My child? Am I his father? darst thou speake it?
Ar. Be not ouer much asham'd on't S^{r}. Yo^{u} are not the
first graue Cittizen, that has got an Ideot
Tes. Here's good stuffe towards.
Buz. Ha ha ha. Hay toodle loodle loodle loe.
Qui. How should I get him? I was neuer maried
till this month.
Ar. How doe other bawdy batchelors get bastards
Tes. Haue yo^{u} bene a bastard getter, and then marry
My neece.
Ed. Now it workes.
Tes. I'll teach yo^{u} to get a bastard sirah.

103. *rock*] staff of a hand-operated spinning wheel, on which wool or flax is placed to be spun.

104. *spindle*] the rounded, slender rod, used in hand spinning, which pulls the wool or flax from the rock and twists it into thread.

113. Child natrall] illegitimate; simple-minded from birth.

Buz. Hay toodle loodle loodle looe.
Qui. Well gentlemen, to take yor wonder off,
I am content to lay truth open to yo^{u}.
For a poore man, a Servant that I had
I payd for keeping of an Ideot
Tis like that this is it. But for a certaine sōme
W^{ch} I did pay, twas articled that I
Should neuer more be trobled wth it.
Tes. Now! What say yo^{u} to that S^{r}?
Ar. Tis not deny'd S^{r}. There was such agreement.
But he is now become another kind of Chardge
Ed. Why he gets something towards his living me thincks
By spinning looke yo^{u}.
Ar. Yes; he has learn'd to thrip among the Mothers;
But S^{r} wthall to doe more harme then good by't.
And that's the chardge I speake of. We are not bound
To keepe yor child, and yor childs children too.
Tes. How's that?
Ar. S^{r} by his cunning at the Rock
And twirling of his spindle on the thripskins
He has ferkt vp the bellyes of Sixteene
Of his Thrip-Sisters.
[*Buz.*] Hey toodle loodle loodle looe.
Tes. Ist possible?
Ar. Soe well he takes after his father it seemes.
Vin. Take heed o'that frend. Yo^{u} heard him say
It was his man's child.
Ar. He sha'nt fright me wth that allthough ta be
A great mans part to turne ouer his bastards
To his Servants (Thanck yo^{u} for yor good will
How euer Gentleman) But I know what I say; [24^{r}]
And I know what I come about, and not wthout
Advise: And moreouer, that *Norfolk* is not wthout

148. *Buz.*] *Ar. MS.*

144. cunning] skill.
145. thripskins] animal hides (?); pudenda.
146. ferkt vp] set in motion; impregnated.
158. Advise] probably legal advice, a reference to the litigiousness of Norfolk people. (See note, III.i.130–31.)

As knauish Councell as another County may be.
Let his man *Buzzard* be brought forth, & see
What he will say to't.
Buz. Hay toodle loodle &c.
Qui. Wretch that I was to put away that fellow.
But stay! Where is my wife, my wife, my wife?
Ed. What say yo^{u} S^{r}?
Qui. My Moore I would say. W^{ch} way went my Moore
Buz. Hay toodle loodle &c.
Vin. Yo^{r} *Ethiopian* Princesse? Nat is gone to daunce
Wth her in private.
Ed. Because yo^{u} laught him out of countenance here.
Qui. Mischiefe vpon mischiefe! Worse & worse. I feare—
Tes. What doe yo^{u} feare? Why stare yo^{u}? Are yo^{u} frantick?
Qui. I must haue witts & fitts; my fancies & fagaries.
Vin. Yo^{r} Iieres vpon poore gallants.
Ed. How doe yo^{u} feele yo^{r}selfe?
Buz. Hey toodle loodle &c.
Ar. Ask yor father blessing *Timsy*.
Buz. Hay toodle loodle &c.
Ar. Vpon yor knees man.
Buz. Vpon all a knees. Ah—ah. toodle loodle.
Enter Nathaniell & Phillis pulld in by the Moore-actor
Nat. What wast to yo^{u}, yee slaues? must yo^{u} be peeping.
Tes. What's the matter now?
Nat. What wast to yo^{u}?
Actor. It is to vs S^{r}. We were hir'd to daunce, and to speake
Speeches; and to doe the gentleman Service in his house:
And not to see his house made a bawdy house, and
make noe speech o'that.
Tes. What is the busines?
Actor. Marry S^{r}, a naughty busines. This gentleman has
Comitted a deed of darknes wth yor Moore here.
We all saw it.
Tes. What deed of darknes? Speake it plainely.

159. knauish Councell] In spinning, a "knave" is "the contrivance in which a spool or spindle revolves" (*OED*); thus, the phrase may extend the analogies between spinning and sex. "Knave" also meant "rascal," however, and with "Councell" likely refers to roguish lawyers or their advice; the phrase "Norfolk lawyer" was synonymous with "clever swindler" (Sugden).

173. fancies] whims.

173. fagaries] vagaries.

Act: Darknes, or Lightnes, call it what yo^{u} will
They haue lyen together.
Qui. Vndone: most wretched. O I am confounded.
I see noe art can keepe a woman honest.
Nat. I loue her, & will iustify my act
Phi. And I thee best of any liuing man.
Nat. Thou speakst good english now.
Qui. O ruine, ruine ruine.
Vin. Why take yo^{u} on soe for an ougly feind.
Qui. She is my wife Gentlemen.
Omnes. How! yor wife.
Qui. My lawfull wife. Yo^{r} Neece. And soe disguisd
by me, on purpose—
Tes. I said he was mad before. ha ha ha.
Nat. Now I applaud my act, twas sweet & braue.
Qui. I'll be divorc'd in publique.
Tes. Now will I vse Authority & skill.
Frends guard the dores, & call a stronger watch
Vse my name in it. None shall depart the house. *Ex^{t} Actors.*
Nat. Vin. Ed. Good S^{r} content.
Ar. Shall I s^{r}, and my Chardge stay too.
Tes. Marry s^{r} shall yee. [24^{v}]
Buz. I feare we shall be smok'd then.
Ar. Noe, noe feare nothing.
Tes. Huswife, yo^{u} know yor Chamber. I'll wayt
On yor master to night. And find lodgings for
Yo^{u} Gentlemen.
Buz. And for vs a Chimney corners.
Tes. We will not part, till, by tomorrow day,
Iustice & Law lights euery one his way.
Vin. Is this the merry night?
Qui. Oh—oh—oh—
Ed. Why roare yo^{u} soe?
Nat. It is the Cuckolds howle; a common cry
About the Citty.
Buz. Hay toodle loodle loodle looe *Ex^{t} oẽs.*

Finis Actus quarti.

212. *Nat. Vin. Ed.*] *inserted after the line of speech was written MS.*

215. smok'd] discovered.

Act. V. Scœne. i.

Meanwell. Rashly. Winlosse. Host.

Mea. Now my good *Host*, since yo^{u} haue bene o^{r} Frend;
And onely Councell keeper in o^{r} absence;
(To wch yo^{u} readily fitted vs wth horses),
To yo^{u}, before we visit our owne houses,
Will giue a true relation of o^{r} Iourney,
And what the motiue was that drew vs forth.
Tis true we did pretend a deadly quarrell
At a great bowling match vpon *Black-heath*;
Went off; tooke horse; and seuerall wayes; forecast
To meet at *Douer*; where we met good frends;
And in one Barque past ouer into *France*:
Here twas supposd to fight, like fashion followers,
That thither fly, as if noe land but that
Could dry vp English blood.
Host. Now by the way
Suppose that supposition had bene true,
And the supposed deathes of yo^{u} & yo^{u}
Had mou'd yor Sonnes to combat in earnest,
And both bene killd indeed, as yo^{u} in Iest
Where had bene then yor witty Subtiltie
My noble *Meanwell*, & my braue *Rashly*
Ha! haue I twight yee there? ah ha!
Rash. Thou keepst thy humor still my riming host.
Host. My humor was, nor is, nor must be lost.
But to my question: was it wisely done
When each of yo^{u} might soe haue lost a Sonne?
Rash. We had noe feare of that S^{r}, by the Rule,
The common Rule o'the world. Where doe yo^{u} find
Sonnes that haue liues & Lands will venter both
For theyr dead Fathers, that are gone & car'd for? [25^{r}]
Nor was it onely to make triall of
What husbands they would be; how spend or saue;

10. *Black-heath*] one of the commons sometimes used for sporting events; situated five miles southeast of the center of London.

24. twight] twit.

25. riming] The references to rhyme here and in line 68 are missing in *O*, probably because a compositor misread "riming" as "running" and "rime" as "ruine"; none of the critics, in studying the text, has divined Brome's purpose or suggested that the host and his humor are meant to be amusing.

How mannage or destroy; how one or both
Might play the Tyrants ouer their poore Tenants
Yet fall by prodigalitie into the Compter.
And then the dead, by doffing a false beard,
After alitle chiding, & some whining,
To set the living on their Leggs agen,
And take them into fauour. pish old Play-plotts.
Noe S^{r} our busines ran another course.
Know yo^{u} this Gentleman yet?
Host. Nor yet, nor yet, nor yet.
Best witts may haue worst Memories. I forget.
Win. It is my part to speake. Mine host yo^{u} haue knowne me.
My name is *Winlosse*, a poore Gentleman:
Yet richer, by my Libertie, then I was
For 6 yeares space, till these good Gentlemen
(Whose names are enterd in the booke of Heauen)
For Charitie redeem'd me
Host. Master *Winlosse*!
I thought I could as soone forgot my Criss-Crosse.
Yet pardon me yo^{u} haue six yeares bene gone;
And all of them in prison saving one,
In *Dunkerke* as I weene.
Win. It is most true;
And that from thence these Gentlemen redeem'd me,
At their owne chardge, by paying fiue hundred pound
W^{ch} was my Ransome
Host. Tis a rare example
Win. Worthy brasse tables, & a Pen of steele
Mean. Noe more, good neighbour *Winlosse*; what we did

37. Compter] general name for any city prison for debtors.

45. Best . . . Memories] "Good wits have bad memories" (Tilley, W577).

53. Criss-Crosse] Christ-cross, the cross figure placed before the alphabet in children's hornbooks; used as a synonym for the alphabet.

56. *Dunkerke*] Dunkirk, town on the Straits of Dover in France that was controlled at various times during the Renaissance by the English, the Spanish (at the time of the play), and the French; it was associated with privateers, prostitutes, and war (Sugden). (Brome does not explain Winlosse's imprisonment—it is not necessary to the plot that we know the cause—but perhaps the mention of Dunkirk would have been enough to suggest to a Caroline audience that Winlosse had been aboard one of the merchant ships overtaken by privateers; this is speculation, but dramatic references to such activity are numerous.)

56. weene] ween, believe or surmise.

62. brasse tables, & a Pen of steele] brass tablets and a steel engraving tool; i.e., worthy to be remembered forever.

Was to dischardge our Conscience of a burden
Got (and twas all we got) by yor vndoing
In a sad suit at Law.
Host. I doe remember.
And wthout Rime I'll tell yo^{u}. That sad cause,
In wch yo^{u} ioynd against him, ouerthrew him
And all his Family. But this worthy Act
Of yo^{r}s, in his inlargement, crownes yor Pietie,
And putts him in a way of better Fortune,
Then his first tottering estate could promise.
Rash. Shut vp that point. Yo^{u} haue heard noe ill yo^{u} say
Among o^{r} Sonnes & Daughters in o^{r} absence
Host. Not any S^{r} at all. But, m^{r} *Winlosse*,
Yo^{u}, that haue past soe many sorrowes, can
Heare one, (I make noe doubt) wth manly patience.
Win. Tis of my daughter *Phillis*—Is shee dead?
Host. Tis well, and't be noe worse wth her. I feare
Shee's gone the tother way of all flesh.
Mea. Peace.
Rash. What a foule beast art thou to tell a Father this?
Host. To haue him right his Daughters wrong
Vpon the fouler beast, that has seduc'd her.
Rash. Who is it? Canst thou tell?
Host. Euen the ranke Rider of the Towne S^{r}. One [25^{v}]
M^{r}. *Nathaniell Banelasse*, if yo^{u} know him.
Mean. He was my sonnes acquaintance
Rash. And mine's too.
Host. Yo^{u} may be proud on't, if they haue scap'd his doctrine
Win. But dos he keepe my daughter to his Lust
Host. Noe S^{r}. Tis worse then soe. he has cast her off,
To the Common, as tis fear'd.
Win. O wretchednes!
Rash. How camst thou by this knowledge?
Host. I haue in the house a Guest, was once yor Man
Mean. My man?

65. Got] Our Co Got ("Our Co" *deleted*) *MS*. 75. o^{r} absence] yor absence *MS*; our *O*.
84. Daughters] Fathers Daughters ("Fathers" *deleted*) *MS*.

81. way of all flesh] Tilley, W166.

Host. Yes S^{r}, and serv'd yor sonne since yo^{u} went ouer
Though now he has got a young sparke to his Master,
That has a brace of Gueldings in my stable
And lusty ones they are. That's by the way
Rash. Pray thee to the point.
Host. S^{r}, the young Gallant is abroad; the Man
Scults close in the house here; & has done these ii dayes.
Sometimes he spends his time wth me in drinck & talke.
And most of his talke runs vpon wenches mainely
And he told me the tale that I told yo^{u}
Twixt *Banelasse* & yor done & vndone daughter. *Ent: Rafe.*
Ra: Mine host—Cry mercy gentlemen.
Mean. Nay come on.
Host. I told yo^{u} he was very shy to be seene.
Ra: My old Master aliue agen! And he that killd him too.
Mean. Whome doe yo^{u} serue? Was I soe ill a Master
That in my absence yo^{u} forsooke my children?
Or how haue they misvsd yo^{u}? Why dost looke
Soe like an apprehended theife? I feare
Thou servst some Robber, or some Murderer
(By what I heare), or art become thy selfe one.
If soe the deuill haue possest thee striue
To turne him out. I'll ad my prayers to helpe thee.
What is the Matter?
Ra. O, honord Master I'll keepe nothing from yo^{u}.
There is an act of horror, now on foot,
Vpon Reuenge of yor supposed Murder:
Of wch to stand, & tell the Circumstance
Would wast the time might hinder the prevention
Of yor sonnes Murder—and yor daughters ruine.
Oẽs. O fearefull
Ra. Let not yor amazement drowne
Yo^{r} Reason, to beget delay. Yo^{r} hast
Was neuer soe requir'd as now. Stay not
To aske me why, or whither. As yee goe
I shall informe yo^{u}.
Ras. Mean. Goe wee'll follow thee. *Ex^{t} oẽs*

105. Scults] skulks.
127. might hinder] *O* reads "and hinder"; a comma after "time" would serve the same purpose.

Scœne. ii. Dionisia sola.

What a fierce Conflict twixt Reuenge & Loue
(Like an vnnaturall ciuill warre) now rages
In my perplexed brest. There, fight it out.
To it, *pelmel* my thoughts. The Battell's hot.
Now for the day! Reuenge beginnes to stagger.
And her distracted Army at an instant [26r]
Rowted, & put to flight. All conquering *Loue*
Thou hast got the victory; And now I sue
(Like a rent kingdome by selfe opposite thoughts)
Vnto thy Soueraigntie to be thy Liege-right.
Take me to thy protection, kingly *Loue*;
And, having captiuated my Reuenge,
O, play not now the Tyrant. A firme hope
Perswades me noe: But when I shall reveale
My selfe, I shall obtaine *Theophilus* loue;
Wch now is ten times sweeter in my thought
Then my Reuenge was when twas first begot. *Ent: Theophilus Lucy.*
The. What! still alone? we haue bene seeking thee.
Dio. O, tis the service that I owe to you Sr.
Lu. Indeed you are too pensiue. Two whole dayes
And nights among vs; and noe more familier?
Knowing how oft my brother & my selfe
Haue tenderd our most true affection to you.
Ent. Page wth Arthure in his false beard & Millicent in a vayle.
Page. May I craue yor name Sr?
Art. That's to litle purpose.
My busines is the thing. Yonder's the starre
What gentleman is that her arme's soe curteous to?
Page. One she thincks well on Sr. Noe matter for his name
Sr, here's a gentleman desires to speake wth you.
The. Dost thou not know his name?
Page. He will not tell it Sr.
The. You treacherous boy. Doe you bring you know not whome

5. *pelmel*] in a disorderly or reckless manner, usually referring to close and heavy combat.

7. distracted] out of ranks; divided.

11. Liege-right] vassal whose loyalty is sworn to a lord.

15. But] but that.

Vnto my priuacie?
Art. My blessed chardge draw neare
The. That gentleman
I was soe bound to sister, yet vnknowne.
The wellcomst man aliue. Thancks my good boy.
What's shee he brings in vayld, and this way leads?
Art. S^{r}, though I am still a stranger in my visit,
To workes of gentlenes I am partly knowne.
There (if yo^{u} chance to inquire of me hereafter,
When I shall more deserue yor inquisition)
I may be found (though not exact in service)
At least a poore Pretender in my wishes.
And soe presenting this white guift (more modest
Then the most secret duty of mans frendship
Euer can be) I take my Leaue.
The. This Man
Would breed, at euery time hee's seene, a wonder.
S^{r} leaue me not thus lost. Let me once know yo^{u};
And what this mistery meanes. This beares a shape
I may not entertaine. I haue set my vow
Against all womankind, since Heauen was married
To my first Loue; and must not willfully
Discouer a temptation wth mine owne hand.
Art. How shie, & nice we are to meet o^{r} happines!
Lyke dying wretches, 'fraid to goe to rest.
Becaus yo^{u} shall be guilty of noe breach,
I'll ope the Casket to yo^{u}. *(He vnvayles her*
The. Blesse me—tis— *and slips away. Ex*
Warme, soe Loue cherish me, & comfortable.

35. priuacie] prau priuacie ("prau" *deleted*) *MS.* 62. SD *Ex*] *runs off the page MS.*

47–49. (more . . . be)] The note may modify the "guift" or the "I" that follows, in the latter case emphasizing Arthur's wish to remain unknown.

58. nice] punctilious; i.e., Theophilus is "nice" in that he is being scrupulously faithful to Millicent, so faithful that he won't unveil her.

61. Casket] The word is used metaphorically and does not imply, as Richard Jefferson suggests, that Arthur brings the supposedly deceased Millicent "to the grieving Theophilus in a casket" (Jefferson, "Some Aspects of Richard Brome's Comedies of Manners," 48). The metaphor is particularly apt, both in the sense of *casket* as something that hides the dead (here the supposedly dead) and in the sense of *casket* as something that contains a jewel (as Brome used the word in IV.iii.95–96).

63. comfortable] tranquil; capable of giving or receiving comfort.

Dio. O death! my hopes are blasted.
Lu: How is it wth yo^{u} S^{r}.
The. Might a Man credit his owne sences now, [26^{v}]
This were my *Millicent.* How thinck yo^{u} Sister?
Mil. Indeed I am soe my *Theophilus.*
Lu. Pray S^{r} how doe yo^{u}?
Dio. Well, well.
Lu. Yo^{u} are not well. Yo^{r} cullor alters strangely
Dio. Giue me ayre then.
Lu. Hee's either ouer-ioyd his cosen liues
Or ells he feares tis but an apparition.
Dio. Shee liues. And he is lost to me foreuer
Loue thou hast dealt falsely wth me; and Reuenge
I reinvoke thy nobler Spirit.
Lu. Brother, how stand yo^{u}? Noble Lady, speake to him.
Mil. I was, in my discouerie, too sodaine
Lu. Strong rapture of his Ioy, I feare, hath cras'd him
Mil. S^{r}, be not wonder-struck; or if yo^{u} be
Let me coniure yo^{u}, by the loue yo^{u} bore me,
Returne vnto yo^{r}selfe againe. Let not
A wandring thought fly from yo^{u}, to examine
From whence, or how I came. If I be wellcome,
I am yor owne, & *Millicent.*
The. And, in that,
Soe blest a treasure, that the wealth & strength
Of all the world shall neuer purchace from me.
Heauen may be pleasd againe to take thee. But
I'll hold soe fast, that wee'll goe hand in hand.
Besides, I hope, his mercy will not part vs.
But where's the man, now more desir'd then euer
That brought yo^{u} hither?
Mil. Yo^{u} aske in vaine for him.
I can resolue yo^{u} all. He past his Service.
I know his mind. He will be knowne by noe man
And me he hath inioynd to silence him.
The. This is a cruell goodnes, to put Thanckfullnes
Out of all action. Sirah, how went he?
Page. I know not S^{r}. He vanishd sodainly.
The. Vanish'd! Good *Lucy*, helpe to hold her fast:

Shee may not vanish too. Spirits are subtle things.
Mil. This was my feare.
The. Fly sirah, ouertake him. *Ext Page.*
Mil. S.r settle but yor patience
And I haue a story will make all things easy.
The. I'll be as calme, in my extreamest deepes,
As is the Couch, where a sweet Conscience sleepes *They set him downe in a Chaire.*
Dio. Tis now determinate as Fate,
And soe
At the whole cluster of hem— *As shee is presenting her Pistoll*
Blesse me! ha! *Enter Rashly. Meanwell. Winlosse*
My father living! Then the cause *Arthure* wthout his false beard. *Rafe*
Is dead, of my Reuenge.
Rash. What! Is he killd outright? or ells but hurt?
Theophilus! my boy! dead past recouery.
Hold fast the Murderesse. Looke you Sr to her. *(Dionisia kneeles to her Father*
Yor sonne too, had a hand in't, I suspect
By the great hast we met him in from hence.
Lu. He is not hurt at all, my honor'd father,
As I desire yor blessing.
But stricken wth an extasy of Ioy
As you shall presently perceaue.
Rash. *Theophilus*! [27r]
Looke vp my boy. How dost? here's none but frends.
The. Sure, sure we all are in *Elizium* then;
Where all are frends; and filld wth equall Ioy.
Earth can haue noe felicitie like this,
If this be any thing.
Rash. Thou canst not thinck vs nothing
Looke well about thee man.
The. I see, I feele, I heare, & know you all.
But who knowes what he knowes, sees, feeles or heares?
Tis not an Age for man to know himselfe in.
Rash. He is not mad I know by that.

108. deepes] deep regions of emotion or thought; cf. *the depths.*

111. determinate as Fate] "As sure as Fate" (Tilley, F81).

The. If I know any thing, yo^{u} are my Father.
Rash. Thou art a wise child.
The. And I beseech yor blessing.
Rash. Thou hast it. *Millicent*, I haue heard yor story.
And *Lucy* yo^{u} betwixt yo^{u} sooth his fancy.
He will be well anon. Keepe'hem company *Arthure*.
And, *Lucy*, bid him wellcome.
Lu. More then health S^{r}.
Rash. Yo^{u} *Dionisia* would be chid alitle
But let me intreat her pardon.
Mean. Dry yor Eyes: yo^{u} haue it.
Goe instantly, resume yor sexes habit;
And, wth the rest, be ready, if we call yo^{u}
To *Quicksands* house. The Rumor of o^{r} coming
Allready calls vs thither, to be assistant
To Iustice *Testy*, in a pondrous difference.
Wayt on yor Mistres sirah; and be honest
Ra: Now will shee beat me euen to death in priuate. *(Ex^{t} Dion: Rafe.*
Rash. Now, how dos he?
Art. Hee's fallen into a slumber.
Rash. In wth him all I pray; And m^{r} *Winlosse*
Yo^{u} are well read in phisique.
Win. I'll take care. *(Ex^{t} wth Theoph.*
Manent Rash. & Meanwell.
Rash. Come my frend *Meanwell.* Now for *Quicksands* cause
To keepe it out of wrangling Lawyers Iawes.
The face of daunger is allmost made cleane;
And may conclude all in a Comick Scene. *Ex^{t} Amb.*

Scœne. iii. Enter Vincent. & Edmond.

Vin. What a foule house is here!
Ed. The master weary & asham'd to owne it.
Vin. Or any thing that's in it, I hope, and soe
He may remit o^{r} Mortgages againe.
Ed. He will be hangd first. Tis not his forwardnes

138–39. "It is a wise child that knows his own father" (Tilley, C309).
154. honest] virtuous, upright.

Scene iii

3. owne] admit (weariness); possess (the house).

To be divorc'd from his wife can perswade me
He will part wth his wealth soe.
Vin. What rich luck
Had that bold venturer *Nat*, to fall vpon her
If he may haue her now.
Ed. Who could haue thought,
That subtle Iew, now cheated in his craft
Would haue disguisd soe sweet a beauty soe?
Vin. She servd him in his kind for't.
Ed. Sure there is
Some further trick in't. We shall see anon.
Old *Testy* will bring all about. He now
Is in his kindgome; ouer head & eares
In raging waues of rough Authority.
Vin. He comes. And his two graue Assistants wth him.
I mervaile how their Sonnes haue wellcom'd them *Ent: Testy* [27^{v}]
In their returne from death. *Rashly.*
Tes. My worthy frends, y'are come vnto a Cause, *Meanwell. they Sitt.*
As rare, as was yor vnexpected coming
From the supposed graue.
Rash. But to the point I pray.
Tes. How quick yo^{u} are! Good m^{r} *Rashly*, know
(Though I crau'd yor Assistance), onely I
Supply the place here of Authority.
Rash. And much good do't yo^{u}. I haue other busines.
Tes. How's that?
Rash. Yo^{r} Neece, S^{r}, was too good for my poore sonne
Tes. How now!
Mean. Nay gentlemen, yo^{u} came to end a busines
Pray first beginne noe new ones.
Rash. Well. I haue done.
[*Tes.*] The first braunch of the question rises here.
Whether *Quicksands* wife my Neece be dead or living?
(Bring in the parties). Speake yo^{u} Gentlemen.
Vin. He did affirme to vs that shee was dead.

24. SD *they*] *interlined with a caret MS.* 29. Assistance), onely] Assistance, I onely ("I" *deleted*) *MS*. I added the closing parenthesis for clarity. 38. *Tes.*] *Mean. MS.* (See "Collation" for the *O* reading of this speech.)

Ed. Though since in a destracted passion
He sayes shee liues.
Ent Quicksands Nathaniell & Phillis
Quic. Shee liues; and is that strumpet
From whome I sue to be divorc'd.
Mean. That *Moore*?
Did yo^{u} wed her since yor faire wiues decease?
Quic. Still it is shee; and all the wiues I had.
That black is but an artificiall tincture,
Layd by my Iealousie vpon her face.
Rash. This is most strange.
Nat. Brauer & brauer still.
I aym'd but at a Clowd, and clasp'd a *Iuno.*
Will yo^{u} be onely mine?
Phil. I haue sworne it, euer.
Nat. Then I am made foreuer
Tes. Remoue her; and let instant tryall be made
To take the blacknes off.
Quic. Then if her shame
And my faire truth appeare not, punish me.
Tes. How euer yor consent to be divorc'd
From *Millicent* my Neece is irrevocable
Quic. Before yo^{u} all I'll forfeit my estate
If euer I reaccept her.
Ras. Then shee is free
Tes. Now m^{r} *Banelasse*
Nat. Now for the honor of wenchers
Test. Yo^{r} fact is manifested, & confest
Nat. In fewest words it is.
Tes. Are yo^{u} content
To take this woman now in question,
If shee be found noe *Moore* to be yor wife,
In holy mariage, to restore her honor?
Nat. Or ells, before yo^{u} all, let me be torne
To peeces, hauing first those dearest Members,
In wch I haue most delighted, dawbd wth honey

59. shame] shame & my ("& my" *deleted*) *MS.* 72 wife,] wife? (*upper part of question mark deleted and lower part changed to a comma*) *MS.*

53. An allusion to the Ixion/Hera (Juno) myth.

To be lickd off by the beares.
Tes. This protestation
Is cleare wthout respect of portion, now,
Or that shee is my Neece: For yo^{u} must know
Shee is noe Neece of mine, that could transgresse
In that lewd kind: nor must shee euer looke
For fauour at my hands. [28^{r}]
Nat. I am content
To take her, as shee is; Not as yor Neece,
But, as his counterfeit Servant. Hoping yet
Hee'll giue me, wth her, all shee beares about her.
Quic. My chaines & Iewells, worth a thousand pounds
I'll pay it for my folly.
Nat. Twill be twise
The price of my pawnd goods. I'll put the rest
Vp, for yor Iieres, past on my frends & mee.
Mean. Yo^{u} are agreed.
Nat. To take her wth all faults. *Ent Phillis (white.*
Phil. I take yo^{u} at yor word.
Quic. hah.—
Nat. Hell, & her changes!
Phil. Lead by the hope of Iustice, I am bold
To fixe here, fast; here, to repaire my ruines
Nat The deuill lookes ten times worse wth a white face
Giue me it black againe.
Phil. Are we not one yo^{u} know, from the beginning?
Nat. Get thee from me. I'll nippe thee dead else
In private & soe leaue thee.
Tes. Sir, Sir, yo^{u} haue yor suit & yor desert.
Tis yor best part to passe it patiently
Rash. Tis *Winlosse* daughter; we haue found the error.
Quic. I am confounded here. Where is my wife?
Rash. I, that's the point must now be vrg'd. The Law
Asks her at yor hands.
Test. Answere quickly sirah.
Quic. I am at my Ioyes end, and my witts together

91–92. put the rest / Vp] keep.
100. "The white devil is worse than the black" (Tilley, D310); possibly also a reference to Webster, *The White Devil* (1612).
103. nippe] pinch, squeeze; sharply bite.
112. witts] "He is at his wit's end" (Tilley, W575).

Mean. Yo^{u} haue brought her fame in question; tis reueng'd.
Now yo^{u} are in both for her life & honor.
Rash. Come to the point. Where is she? Answere briefly
Tes. Speake Villaine, Murdrer, speake, where is my Neece?
Quic. I haue snar'd my selfe exceeding cunningly.
That Queane, there, knowes.
Nat. Take heed S^{r} what yo^{u} say.
Shee's thought to be my wife. Hands off I pray.
These are my goods shee weares. Giue me'hem *Phill.*
For feare he snatch. I'll put'hem in my pocketts.
Phil Sweet heart, mine owne will hold hem.
Nat. Sweet-heart allready? yo^{u} are soone famillier.
Phil. Yo^{u} haue bene soe wth me: we are noe strangers.
Rash. Well m^{r} *Quicksands*, (though yo^{u} cannot answere)
To put yo^{u} by the feare of halter-stretching,
Since yo^{u} haue ingag'd yor word & whole estate
To be devorc'd; and yo^{u}, good m^{r} *Testy*,
If you'll be willing yet that my poore Sonne
Shall wed yor Neece, as I shall find it Lawfull,
I'll vndertake her safe recouery.
Tes. I haue in heart giuen her yor Sonne allready.
Thus I confirme it.
Rash. And he has her allready. *Ent. Theophilus & Millicent, Arthure & Lucy Winlosse Dionisia.*
As for example, see s^{r}.
Quic. See, See, the heauen that I am iustly fallen from
O may I yet find fauour.
Mil. Neuer here
Hadst thou not giuen thy faith to a diuorce;
On forfeiture of thine estate, (wch thou
Dost hold more precious) or couldst now redeeme
That great ingagement; and then multiply [28^{v}]
Thy vast estate into a ten-fold Somme;
Make me Inheritrix of all; and last assure me
To dy wthin a weeke I would not remarry thee.
Adulterate beast, that brokst thy former wedlock
In thy base lust wth that thy Servant there.
Nat. What a pox, noe I troe! My wife that must be

118. Queane] quean, hussy or harlot.

Phil. Twas yor owne doing to put me to my shifts
Nat. The deuill shift yo^{u}, then yo^{u} shall be sure
Of change enough.
Win. O shame vnto my blood!
Nat. I will henceforward councell all my frends
To wed their whores at first, before they goe
Out of their hands
Tes. How can yo^{u} answere this?
Quic. I vtterly deny't vpon my oath.
Phil. Soe doe I; & safely, for any act.
It was but in attempt. Nothing in act I assure yo^{u}.
Nat. In him twas foule enough though.
Mean. O hatefull vice in Age!
Tes. Tis an old Vice growne in him from his youth
Of wch bring forth the example. Where's his bastard?
Buz. I feare we shall be whipt for counterfets *Ent: Arnold*
My long Coates haue a grudging of it *Buzzard*
Ar. I see my old masters face againe, & I will feare nothing
Buz. Then I'll beare vp againe.
Hay diddy daddy, play wth thy babby
Dindle dandle on thy knee, & giue him a penny } Sing.
And a new Coat o hoe—
Quic. My griefe & shame is endles
Vin. Let not griefe Master yo^{u} m^{r}. *Quicksands*:
We are yor frends & pitty yor afflictions
What will yo^{u} giue vs now; & wee'll release yo^{u}
Foreuer of this changeling charge of yo^{r}s
Ed. And proue hee's not yor bastard. Speake now: Roundly.
Quic. I'll cancell both yor forfeit Mortgages
Vin. A Match. Now looke yo^{u} S^{r}. Yo^{r} *quondam* Servant
All but the goodly beard he wore, for w^{ch}
We are to giue him a large recompence
Quic. O *Buzzard Buzzard, Buzzard.*
Buz. O master, master, Master.
Yo^{r} Servant, & noe bastard;
Nor father of yor Ideot in *Norfolke*

150. shifts] stratagems; a "shift," however, was also a chemise, and Nat's reply (line 151) involves this meaning of the word: "A basic sense of *shift*, n. and v., is 'a change' . . . —present both in the 'trick' and in the 'chemise' sense" (Partridge).

166. it] i.e., the whipping. *O* reads "the lash" for "it."

Hee's there & well Sr. I heard lately of him.
Quic. How couldst thou vse me thus?
Buz. How could you turne me away.
Test. Come hither *Buzzard*; thou shalt not want a Master.
Arn. Nor I, (I hope) while my old master liues.
Y are wellcome home Sr.
Rash And thou to me my good old Servant *Arnold.*
Quic. Well fare a Misery of a mans owne seeking;
A tough one, that will hold him tack to his end.
This comes wth wiuing at threeskore & three
Would doating fooles were all servd soe for me.
Tes. To shut vp all: *Theophilus*, take my Neece.
Wee'll shortly find a lawfull course to marry her. [29r]
Rash. I will take care for't. *Arthure*, take my daughter
Wth a glad fathers blessing
Mean. And mine wth it: wishing my daughter were

192. *Rash*] *Rash* (*written over "Quic."*) *MS.*

194. tough] stiff, severe.

194. tack to his end] keep him moving in a course contrary to the end he hopes for; be a match for him until his end or the end; see Tilley, T7.

198. lawfull course] Accounts of English matrimonial law differ and sometimes contradict each other, but a playwright as astute as Brome would not have indicated that Theophilus and Millicent would be united if the members of his audience, aware of the laws at least generally, would have rejected the action as impossible. Parliamentary divorce did not exist; ecclesiastical divorce was shameful, as Quicksands knew when he cried for a divorce "in publique" (IV.iv.208), and did not allow of remarriage; and as "divorce" was, in any case, sometimes loosely used to mean any permanent separation, divorce would not seem to have been the "lawfull course." Annulment seems the most likely step. The marriage had not been consummated, and though that alone would not have been grounds for annulment, one probably could not have been obtained had this not been the case (or been sworn to be the case). Since Nat refers to Millicent as Theophilus's "betrothed loue" (I.ii.100) and Theophilus says she was his wife "But for the poore bare name of Mariage onely" (IV.ii.26), it is reasonable to believe that a precontract existed, probably a contract *in verbis de praesenti*, which was valid as a marriage, "though not so in name" (Camden, *Elizabethan Woman*, 88). Such a precontract would have been an impediment to another marriage of either party and legitimate grounds for an annulment. William Harrington, in *The Comendacions of Matrimony* (1528), also includes diversity in religion and forced matrimony as impediments (Camden, *Elizabethan Woman*, 92). Most clergymen, however, would be reluctant to invalidate a sacrament—"Wee'll shortly find a lawfull course" indicates that the matter was not clear-cut—but Camden notes: "It was easy enough to bring pressure to bear on the clergy, particularly when persons of wealth and nobility were involved" (Camden, *Elizabethan Woman*, 93); and Testy has said: "If all the Law bodily & Ghostly, / And all the Conscience too, that I can purchace / Wth all the wealth I haue, can take her from him / I will recouer her" (IV.iii.190–93). Caroline matrimonial law can and will be debated; the essential point for the purposes of the play is that Millicent and Theophilus will, somehow, be lawfully united.

As well bestow'd.
Dio. S^{r} take noe thought for me
Till my strict life,
In expiation of my late transgression
Gainst Mayden modestie, shall render me
Some way deserving th'honor of a husband.
Rash. Spoke like a good new woman.
Tes. How now, m^{r} *Banelasse*! Doe yo^{u} looke squeamishly
Vpon yor fortune? S^{r} here's a gentleman shall
Maintayne her blood, as worthy as yor owne
Till yo^{u} defild it Tis good yo^{u} purify't againe.
Nat. Cadzookes I will. pray Giue her S^{r} yor blessing.
Win. I doe, & pray to heauen for blessings on her.
Nat. Vd forgiue me for swearing. I'll turne Puritane
And pray that all my breethren speed noe better.
Phil. My father
Win. O my Child.
Nat. Though m^{r} *Quicksands*
Made a Mock-mariage wth his English Moore
I'll not mock thee. I bobd too much before.
Tes. Enough enough. All pleasd I hope at last,
But m^{r} *Quicksands* here.
Quic. Epilogue. I yeild to Fortune wth an humble knee.
If you be pleas'd, your pleasure shall please mee.
Finis

204. life,] life, by mak ("by mak" *deleted*) *MS*. In *O*, there is an additional line: "(By making man, and the world meer strangers to me,". 213. pray] *interlined with a caret MS*.

215. Vd] ud, minced form of "God."

221. bobd] bobbed, cheated or deceived; copulated, from the motion of bobbing.

224. The *O* epilogue (see "Collation") may have been added at another time—prologues and epilogues were often separate from the text, and new ones were written for new occasions. It would hardly have been politic to include an epilogue with "*to fly from truth, and run the State*" (*O*) in a manuscript intended for William Seymour.

APPENDIX

Collation

Dedication

1–27 *omit*

Prologue

1–29 *omit*; + *Prologue.*
MOst noble, fair and curteous, to ye all
Welcome and thanks we give, that you would call
And visit your poor servants, that have been
So long and pitiless unheard, unseen.
Welcome, you'l say your money that does do,
(Dissembling is a fault) we say so too.
And your long absence was no fault of your,
But our sad fate to be so long obscure.
Jove and the Muses grant, and all good Men,
We feel not that extremity again:
The thought of which yet chills us with a fear
That we have bought our liberty too dear:
For should we fall into a new restraint,
Our hearts must break that did before but faint.
You noble, great and good ones, that vouchsafe
To see a Comedy, and sometimes laugh
Or smile at wit and harmeless mirth, As thus
ye have begun to grace and succour us;
Be further pleas'd (to hold us still upright,
For our relief, and for your own delight)
To move for us to those high powers whom we
submit unto in all humility,
For our proceeding, and we'le make it good
To utter nothing may be understood
Offensive to the state, manners or time,
We will as well look to our necks as climb.
You hear our sute, obtain it if you may;
Then find us money and we'le find you play.
[The prologue refers to the closing of the theaters in 1636–1637 because of the plague; lines 16–28 indicate that the company either had been suppressed or threatened with suppression because of comments in their plays, but nothing is known of the circumstances (Bentley, *The Jacobean and Caroline Stage* 3:68).]

The Persons in the Play

1–22 *omit*; + *Drammatis Personae.*
Meanwell. } *Two old Gentlemen and friends, sup-*
Rashley. } *posed to have been kill'd in a Duel.*
Arthur, Meanwels *Son, in love with* Lucy.
Theophilus, Rashleys *Son, in love with* Milicent.
Quicksands, *an old Usurer.*
Testy, *an old angry Justice.*
Winlose, *a decayed Gentleman.*
Vincent. } *Two gallants undone by* Quicksands.
Edmund. }
Nath. Banelass, *a Wencher.*
Host. *Drawer.*
Ralph, Meanwels *servant.*
Arnold, Rashleys *servant.*
Buzard, Quicksands *servant.*
Dionisia, Meanwels *daughter.*
Lucy, Rashleys *daughter.*
Milicent, Testys *Neece.*
Phillis, Winlose *daughter.*
Madge, Quicksands *servant.*
The Scene *London.*

I.i

9 (Allmost, vpon my life)] (Upon my life) almost
+ But nature has her swing in me. I must.
Therefore I crave you (as you are my brother)
To shake this dull and muddy humor off,
By visiting the streets, and quit your chamber,
Which is a sickness to you.
[Variants from uncorrected formes occur among the copies of the octavo, in line 1 of this addition: me I must. *ICN*, *LL–B*; me I must. I must. *E*.]
12 and haue] I have
21 ofe] over
23 whilst] while
31 vnnaturall] unmanly
34 his] ours
42–47 *Dio.* . . . Sorrow.] *omit*
47 Where's] *Di.* O where's
48 Which . . . on't] That . . . of't
53 Put] stir up / Some
54 might] may
55 Be it] Bee't
58 the] your

59 Onely] Meerly
60–63 *omit*; + *Di.* Is the old Ruffian tane, and hang'd, that slew
My Father; or his son Brain-battered; or
His Daughter made a prostitute to shame?
64 wishes Sister] wishes
68 last me] last
75 *omit*
76 *Theophilus*] *Di. Theophilus*
77 her they say'd.] her.
81 head. And there is sport for yo^u now.] head! More then he would do / For's father, were he hanged, as you did wish / For laughing newes eene now. Ther's sport for you.
89 threeskore od] past three-score
95 now they] they now
104 + I would fain get abroad, yet be unknown.
106 Players beard] false beard which
107 haue put some Iest vpon you in] ha'worn't and put a jest upon
108 [+ SD] Ar. *puts on / the beard.*
111 *Hector* in it] *Hector.*
112 me— *Ex^t. R*] me.
+ *Di.* Be sure you carry a strict eye o're his actions,
And bring me a true account.
Ra. I warrant you Mistriss.
Di. Do, and I'le love thee everlastingly.
113 *Dio.* Why] Why
114 Expect me towards th'euenning. Farewell, Sister— *Ex^t*] Farewel Sister. *Exit.* Ar. Ra.

I.ii

1 *Scene. ii. Enter Nathaniel. &*] ACT I. SCENE 2. / *Nathaniel.*
2 Pray thee be] Prithee be and
3–5 *omit*; + I ha' no more to say to you in the way
You wot on *Phillis.*
Phi. Nor do I seek to you
In that way which you wot on, wanton Sir,
6 require yo^u to be honest, &] be honest, and to
9 that yo^u may liue on] to live upon
10 Y'are] You are
13 Trade-teachers] teachers
15 that the] the poor
19–20 *omit*; + But look not after me: I am not mark'd
For Matrimony, I thank my stars.
29 touch] lie with
31 In *O*, the SD begins at line 32.
32 sought yo^u] sought
35 'bout the] i'the
37 as o^{r}selfes] youthful Gallants
38 That] As

43 pray thee] prithe
47 keepe] hold [+] Pray thee speak; what mischief
+ Is come upon him.
Ed. I pray thee guess again.
Nat. Has somebody over-reach'd him in his way
Of damnable extortion; and he cut his throat,
Or swallowed poison?
Vin. Ten times worse then that too.
Nat. Is he then hoisted into the Star-Chamber
For his notorious practises? or into
The high Commission for his blacker arts?
Ed. Worse then all this.
Nat. Pax, keep it to your self then,
If you can think it be too good for me.
Why did you set me a longing? you cry worse
And ten times worse; and know as well as I,
The worse it is to him, the better wel-come
Ever to me: And yet you tell me nothing.
51 What is shee, ha!] Ha, ha, ha.
52 had had my *Philly*] had my wench
53 shee? quick, what is shee?] she he has married? quickly prithe.
54 him. The] him. / *Ed.* The
57 Hee'll] But he will
58 I'll be sworne] Gentlemen
61 *Ed*] *Vin.*
62 And take vs wth yo^{u} S^{r}. What will yo^{u}] *Ed.* And take us with you. What will you go
63 cannot doe] can
67 *Vin.*] *Ed.*
68 *omit*
70 shame] a shame
75 *omit*
76 The] *Ed.* The
80 had hope to had] claim'd marriage of
83–84 *omit*
86 spoyle all p^{r}sently] prevent us do you think
89 in sooth] ifaith
90 hast] has [+SD] & / Arnold.
93 In *O*, the change of speaker occurs at line 94 with "'Twould."
97 *omit*
98 *Nat.* Gentle] Gentle
99 vs] us all
101–4 *omit*
111 thee . . . yee] you . . . you
112 yor hearts out] you for't
113–14 *omit*; + *Nat.* Zooks what mean you.
Vin. Hold, Sir, forbear.
118 *Ed.*] *Ed. Vin.*
120 merrit is] merit's
121 Wiues] womans
123 her Vndeservings, it were] his undeservings, twere
128 (*Fight againe*] *He hurts / him.*

132–33 *fights / on Theophilis part.*] *sides with* / Theoph. [Theo. *DFo–2.*]
133 *Vin.Ed.*] *Ed.Vin.*
134 oppression] oppression gentlemen
135 *omit*
136 busines] stuff
134–36 In *O*, line 136 precedes line 134.
137–38 is raisd? / Fall back: Twill proue a scirvy busines els.] rais'd? fall off, tis an ill busi- / (ness.
140 I am] I'm
141 *He*] *Arnold*
142–43 *omit*; + *Art.* What fortune's this,
I fought 'gainst friends to save mine enemy,
145 offence] offence to them
148 I am] I'm
152 And] To my remembrance
156 For searching me. Why . . . ?] Why . . . ? I shall be sick to think on't.
157 I am] I'm
158 I am] I'm
162 on] sir
163 The least occasion; and be] On least occasion, and
166 truth] troth
171 old Vncles Will] self willed uncle
176 they would] they'd
177–78 *omit*
180 knowne] know
183 Pish] Push
187 Law] Lawes
189 haue theyr] ha'their
+ Prisons are fill'd with Banckrupts; yet we see
How crafty Merchants often wrong their credits,
And *Lond'ners* flie to live at *Amsterdam!*
191 + And ever incident to the noblest Natures.
196 estate] estates
213 there againe] there
214 find] see
215 wth them] with'em
216 The] Why here's the

I.iii

1 *Scene. iii. Enter*] ACT I. SCENE 3.
13–14 *omit*
15 Loue] *Tes.* Love
16 I will] Ile
20 her then] her
23 Nephue] As I do, Nephew
24 I not doubt] Better I doubt not. Come we shall agree.
30 + I'le see it done. And cause you are so nice
(To bed I say) there I will see more done

Then I will speak. Tell me of your endeavour!

31 Good Vncle be not yo^{u} soe rough & stiffe wth her.] Be not so rough and stiffe with her, good Uncle,

35 but] of

39 *omit*; + *Tes.* 'Tis your sullenness;

40 *Tes.* Would] Would

44 + *Quick.* Indeed the better half; not without hope
To have the rest as he may want my money.

46 + And that wherein she has vext me a thousand times,

55–56 hang about his neck / Ah my *Ioe* ah ha ha.] Ha, my Joe, ha, ha, ha, &c.

57 *omit*; + *Tes.* Hey day.
Quick. She'l make me blush anon I think.

59 *Quic.*] *Tes.*

60–61 Indeed . . . Song as old / As thine owne] That . . . old songs and over old ones, / Old as thy reverend

62 Chick did shee call mee? That's a common word] She cals me chick and bird: The common names

63 + *Mil.* (Shee sings)

65 Sings] [See line 63.]

70 to it] to't

71 + (Shee sings)

72 Sings] [See line 71.]

73 *the*] *thy*

77 day] might [for *n*ight]

79 Will sute] may / Become

81 this] thus

88–89 *omit*; + *Mil.* (She sings.)

90 Sings] [See line 89.]

92 Dee heare me . . . in] Do you hear . . . i'

93 mine] my

97 him? Prithee] him i'bed?

99 Has mortified] Of hers, has outfac'd

100 And dasht me out of] Dasht all quite out o'

102–3 if a preventing witt / Be not in speedy readines? * O] * How now*!* O

103–5 *noyse of / Sowgelders hornes / wthin*] *sowgelders / horn blown*

105 What] *Tes.* What

106 *omit* [In *O*, the SD occurs at line 107.]

108 Whilst] While

110 ouer] ore

112 *omit*; + *Quic.* What they, what all

114 They are . . . of] Their . . . o'

115 giue yee] gi'ye

118 Call out] Call

125 + *Quic.* Tis a flat conspiracy.
This is your bashful modest whimpring Neece.

126 Well] *Tes.* Then

127 hereafter] to morrow

128 *Enter*] *florish, / Ent.*

152–56 *omit*; + Enter four Masquers
with horns on their
heads: a Stag, a
Ram, and Goat, a

an Ox followed by four persons, a Courtier, a Captain, a Schollar and a Butcher.

157 horn-beasts! Wee'll see all] horn beasts.

160 that] who

162 a] that

166 A] That

167 This Enginiere wth Rammes his sconse] The Enginier his sconse with Rams

171 This . . . that] That . . . this

173 the] this

174–77 *omit*

182–83 *omit*; + *They dance to musick of Cornets & Violins.*
The Daunce. Exit. Masquers.

189 Vnlesse some of my husbands frends] Some of my husbands friends perhaps

192–94 *omit*

195 *omit*; + *Mil.* Lock the doors after'em, and let us to bed;

196 vp safe] up, chick, safe from all danger

197 Yes: weell to bed since yo^{u} will] We will to bed chick, since you'l

199 For me . . . in it] Shall secure me . . . in't

200 brought] bring

201 But be] Be

202 thee] thee'gain

204 Impudence] immodestie
+ *Mil.* Thou hast good store of gold, and shalt not want it
In Cullises: in every broth Ile boil
An angel at the least.
Qui. Ile hang first.

205 my witts] wits

206 [+] Heark thee. *They whisper*

207 It is] Tis

210 can bride] bride

212 [+] good!

213 Goe. Will] Will

214 + *Tes.* They wait you in your chamber.
Buz. The devil o'maid's i'this but my fellow *Madg* the Kitching maid, and *Malkin* the Cat, or batchelor but my self, and an old Fox, that my master has kept a prentiship to palliate his palsie.

215 Where be the] *Mil.* Where be the maids, I say; and

216 Doe yo^{u} marke] Mark you

218 husband] Bridegroom

219 To saue his points &] Instead of points, to

221 haue . . . on't] make . . . here

223 talkes] talks so

225 To] Will you to

226 Heigho heigho] Hey ho

228 *omit*

II.i

3 *omit* SD

13 there] there *Phillis*

18 And much] Somewhat

22 ere] ever

27 She trod vpon] I find her.

28 *omit*

30 one litle] at a little

31 a Countrey] Town

32–34 *omit;* +
purge
Out of her while she lives; she smothring it,
And not make known her passion. There's the mischief!

36–37 *omit;* + *Phi.* An enemy! Put case the case were yours.
Lu. But 'tis no case of mine; put by I pray thee.
Phi. I'le put it to you though I miss your case.
Suppose it were your house, and Master *Arthur*,

39 Is] Were

40 I pray thee now] Pray thee

47 + *Lu.* Thou hast won
My patience to attention: Therefore tell me

48 *Lu.* But canst thou] If thou canst

49 foster such] take such an

50 and most] most

52 betwixt] between

56 W^{ch}] That

65 + *Lu.* Thou hast given me strength to tell thee, and I hope
When it is told, I shall have yet more ease.
Phi. I warrant you Mistriss. Therefore out with it.

71 held] bred

88 *omit;* + My Brother being abroad; and such an absence
Has not been usual: I have not seen him

91 In *O*, the SD occurs at line 92.

93 *Lu.*] *Phi.*
+ If no ill accident has happened you
Since your departure; as I fear there has:

94 But why looke yo^{u}] Why looke you else

97 tell me] tell

99 by't. Therefore pray yo^{u} tell me] by't.

109 eene tremble trembles] even tremble-tremble-trembles

115 *omit*

116 What] *Lu.* What

119 + *The.* What do you mean?

120 . . . matches my deare] *Lu.* . . . matches, my good

130 th'aiery] a'ery

133 house to vexe my patience] house

135 has wrought] has

136–37 *omit*; + by councel and discourse wrought much
Ease and delight into my troubled thoughts.

139 gentle Sister] my gentle Sister, / I pray thee

140 fiery] hasty

143 ist] is it

146 (For ought I know) by] By

148 gainst *Arthure* then] then against *Arthur*

152 yo^u, to seeme] your self, / In seeming

158 yor] you

162 *omit*

163 and putts'hem] puts'em

164 + *The.* How quick you are!
Lu. Good Brother I ha'done.

168 Yo^u now are wellcome; though we ꝑted] y'are welcome, though we parted somewhat

171 (I hope (at least)] for I hope

174 of's] of his

175 yo^u . . . before I came] your wonted nature . . . / With me before I could come at you.

176–77 *omit*; + However, I
Have news for you that might deserve your love,
Were you my deadly enemy.

178 is it *Nat*] is't pray thee

179 *Lucy*—] *Lucy* so long unsaluted? *Kiss.*

180 newes] news Sir

182 for] for fear

185 of the right stamp too] o'the right stamp

187 & diuers] with divers

202 bride] wife

203 old wretch will shortly feare] wretch will shortly be afraid

209 Fids; while her old] Fidlers, while her

212 Bride-bed] bride-bed the first night?

213 Marry hang] Hang

214 pusht] put

217 follow't] follow it

222 kill thee] with the safety of my man-hood, / Right me upon that mischievous head of thine.

230 I . . . Iustice] that I . . . Justice on him

235 subtle crueltie] cruelty

238 S^r I can answere yo^u] I answer—

242 heare me then] then

244 Pray S^r, on what acquaintance.] On what acquaintance Sir. [+SD] *He takes / her aside.*

245 on thee] o'thee

247 bitt] bit and th'wilt

251–52 *omit*

254 *omit*; + *Nat.* Pray tell your Master now: so fare you (well Sir. *Exit.*

255 Brother I thanck yo^u] I thank you, Brother,

256 What wast he sayd] some other time / Will be more fit. What said he

258 Helpe] Marry he said (help
259 was't] was it that
+*Phi.* I have it now.
260 *Phil.* Marry he sayd in answere] It was in answer, Sir,
261 whereas yo^{u} feared that . . . man] you fear'd . . . man, wickedly,
262 worcke his faire wiues death] make away his wife: to which he saies
264 Next, that whereas] And next, / That
265 Yo^{u} doubt hee'll] he would
266 He sayes shees] To which he answers, she is
267 lockd] lock'd up
269 Locks of Security, yet as shee is] or security: / Yet being
270 all those] those
272–73 *omit*
278 *Lu:*] *The.*
279 *The.*] *Lu.*
280–82 *omit*; + *Phi.* Yes; I knew that: my wit else had been puzzl'd.
The. And now I find my self instructed by him;
And friends with him again. Now, *Arnold*, any tidings.
281 In *O*, the SD occurs at line 283.
283 Gentleman I sought] gentleman
284–85 *omit*
286 *Ar.* . . . notice] . . . knowledge
287–88 *omit*
289 *Ar.* Yo^{r}] Your
290 now got] got
291 soundly arm'd] weapon'd well
294 Now my] My
295 Let's in to breakfast. *Ex^{t} oẽs*] To dinner sister.

II.ii

1 *Scene*] ACT. 2 Scene
2 a good] good
3 devills wth a Mischiefe!] Devils.
4 It was her villanous plot, & she shall] 'Twas her plot, / And let her
5 *omit*
6 Smart] Smart, Sir,
7 tis] 'twas
9 wedding night] wedding
12 cause] as [+ SD] *Ent. Buz. / with a paper.*
14–16 *omit*
17 *Ex^{t}.*] *Quick. reads it.*
18 + Sawst thou not who convai'd it in?
Buz. Not I. I onely found it, Sr.
19 S^{r}] you
20 out] ow'd
21 + Nay, I that have so many gallant enemies
On fire, to do me mischief, or disgrace;

That I must provide tinder for their sparks!
The very thought bears weight enough to sink me.

22 what trobles yo^{u}] your trouble

25 there] in that letter there

26 that envy me haue tane their] have tane

29 *Qui.*] *Tes.*

30 [+] Pray, Sir, your pa- / (tience,

31 S^{r} I'll . . . will offer] I will . . . endeavour

36 among'hem] amongst'em

45 mine owne; and I am] my own; and i'm

46 mine] my

49 That] Who

52 follies] folly

56 I'ld . . . mine] I would . . . my

66 And I] I

73 ten] twenty

76 his] your

88 + *Tes.* What needs all this?
Do we not live in a well govern'd City?
And have not I authority? Ile take
The care and guard of you and of your house
'Gainst all outragious attempts; and clap
Those Goatish Roarers up, fast as they come.

90 We shall agree I see] Twill put 'em to more trouble,
+ And more expence in doubtful search of her,
The best way to undo 'em is to foil'em
At their own weapons. Tis not to be thought
The'l seek, by violence to force her from me,
But wit; In which wee'l overcome'em.

91 betwixt] twixt

92 *omit*; + I'le leave you to your selves.

93 Now I dare trust thee Neece. Comply still] Heark hither Neece—Now I dare trust you

94 dost thou heare me] hear'st thou girl

107 away I say] now take my journey / Down to my countrey house

108 a . . . againe] your . . . again. No ceremony

110 *Amb.*] *Quic. Mil.*

113 Yo^{u} are] Y'are

116 *omit*

118 Be it] Be't

119 yo^{u} are] y'are

121 *omit*

123 reputation, that] reputation

124 *omit*

126 All will comend yo^{u} for't] They'l commend you for it

137 *omit*

138 yor owne] your

II.iii

1 *Scene*] ACT 2. SCENE
3 *omit*
4 truth] truth: you may believe it, Lady.
5 sillable] sillable more
7 A fit . . . telltruthes] Fit . . . Tell-troths
9 To watch & sift] For watching of
10–11 And bring yo^{u} the account. Yo^{u} . . . / . . . yo^{u} would loue me] You . . . / That you would love me for it
+ *Dio.* Arrogant Rascal.
12 *Dio.* I bid] I bad
15 holpe . . . merciles] help't . . . bloody
16 Was the vntimely end of] Kild
17 [+] My brother doe't*!*
+Or draw a sword to help *Theophilus.*
23 haue but] pray have
24 *a*] *gives her a*
36–38 *omit*
43 + To you I am sweet Lady, and to my master
In true construction: he is his friend I think
That finds his follies out to have them cur'd,
Which you have onely the true spirit to do.
47 on top] o'top
52 in his] in's
58 (*She*] *He offers to / kiss her, she* [In *O*, the SD begins at line 57.]
65 chayre. *(She sitts*] chair.
66–68 *omit;* + *Ra.* The warm touch of my flesh
Already works in her. I shall be set
To better work immediately. I am prevented.
69 *Dio.* Away. My brother comes. But still be] Away and be not seen. Be
71–72 Another time I am] This clinches. Another time I'm [In *O*, the SD in which Arthur enters occurs at line 70.]
73 How] where are you? How [+ SD] *(She sits.* [See line 65.]
74 *omit;* + Sick brother—sick at heart, oh—
83 dear] good
84 suffer it] suffer't
89 know't] know it
90 Yet rather] Rather
95 doe it] do't
107 trembles] tremblest
114 look'd too] look'd, for
115 doe? (*aside*] do?
145 brother. *(She rises.*] Brother.
146 well] cur'd
149 Thou hast] Th'hast
150 on purpose] o'purpose
156 raisd them] rais'd'em
166 [+SD] She tears & / throws the / paper to him.
168 I'll] But
169 though wth] with my
173 *omit*

III.i

6 yor] you

12 could] can

13 + *Buz.* That cursed Mistris that ever she came here!

14 *Buz.* If I knew] If I know

16 [+] because you have lost
+ your wife before she was well found, must we
Poor innocents be quilty?

17 And for] For

19 of the . . . of dore] o'the the . . . o'door

22 *Amb . . . Ex^{t} Amb*] *Buz. Mad . . . Exit*

27 viewing of my] my concealed [In *O*, the SD occurs at line 28.]

32 away] away / With blame enough

37 whilst] while

51 bones. I shake to thinck on'hem.] bones.

58 A] An

67 Tincture is] tincture's

68 lay downe] allay [+ SD] *A box of / black paint- / ing.*

83 I'm] I am

87 white] while

89 when] in
+ In stormy troubled weather no Sun's seen
Sometimes a moneth together: 'Tis thy case now.
But let the roaring tempest once be over,
Shine out again and spare not.
Mil. There's some comfort.
Quic. Take pleasure in the scent first; smell to't fearlesly,
And taste my care in that, how comfortable He begins to
'Tis to the nostril, and no foe to feature. paint her.
Now red and white those two united houses,
Whence beauty takes her fair name and descent,
Like peaceful Sisters under one Roof dwelling
For a small time; farewel. Oh let me kiss ye
Before I part with you—Now Jewels up
Into your Ebon Casket. And those eyes,
Those sparkling eyes, that send forth modest anger
To sindge the hand of so unkind a Painter,
And make me pull't away and spoyle my work,
They will look streight like Diamonds, set in lead,
That yet retain their vertue and their value.
What murder have I done upon a cheek there!
But there's no pittying: 'Tis for peace and honour;

90 Hold . . . amisse] And pleasure must give way. Hold . . . / amiss now by your glass

91 *omit*; + *Mil.* Some humbler habit must be thought on too.

94 *omit*

95 That] *Mil.* And

98 knocks] knock
99–100 *Country / Lasse*] Cook-maid
101 *Quicksands*] *Quick-sands* Sir
102 of the] Here o'the
105 *omit*; + *Phi.* 'Tis upon that, Sir, I would speak Sir, hoping
106 You'll] That you will
109 But a] A
112 folke] folks
116 S^{r} I] I
119 Yes] Yes indeed
120 an Attorney] a Retorney
123 well as] well's
129 in his] in's
130 few Innocents in the County] but few innocents i'the countrey
131 [+] what should
+ That *Hulverhead* be a councellor, Sir.
Quic. No a husband man.
132 *omit*; + *Phi.* Truly I know none.
133 How knewst thou that I want] I am glad she do's not. How knew'st thou I wanted
134 Euen at . . . S^{r} by] At . . . in
135 placeth . . . the] places . . . a
136 That yo^{u} put out] You put away
137 Ah] All
143–45 *omit*; + But very just in all your promises.
146 *Ph.* . . . choose S^{r}] . . . chuse
149 has] hath
150 flesh] ware
152 Whilst] While
154 + *Phi.* May I make bold to crave your ansvver, Sir?
155 Come] *Quic.* Come
157 Hulke] And hulk

III.ii

*[This scene corresponds to the initial section of III.iii in *O*.]
1 *Scœne ii Enter Lucy &*] ACT. 3. SCENE. 3. / *Lucy*
5–7 *omit*
8–10 *omit*; + *The.* I am sorry sister, trust me, truly sorry,
And knew I which way to recover her
With my best care I would. Yet, give me leave,
I saw her overbold; and overheard her
12 Should marry yo^{u} . . . first. *Ent*: *Arnold*] Should be your husband . . . first.
+ *Lu.* Now you fly out again.
The. Your pardon again your sister,

And for your satisfaction I will strive
To oversway my passion. How now *Arnold*, *Ent. Arn.*

13 *omit*
15 yo^{u}, is, The] is, the old
16–18 *omit*; + *Quicksands* has lost his wife.
The. She is not dead,
19 were dead] were
20 might thinck to] then might
21 shee is run away, most roundly] she's run away:
22 *omit*; + But to what corner of the earth, or under
Whose bed to find her is not to be thought.
It has rais'd such a laughter in the town
25–26 haue / heard on't . . . is] hear . . . tis
27 that I] I
28 *omit*; + Out of my doors, thou villain, reprobate.
He beats Arnold.
31 villaine] mischievous Villain
32–33 *omit*; + *Lucy* Is not this passion, brother?
The. Forbear, sister.
37 *omit*
38 *omit*; + Or villain, look to die, oft as I see thee. *Ext. The. Lu.*
39–46 *omit*

III.iii

*[This scene corresponds to III.ii in *O*.]
1 *Scœne iii Enter. Drawer.*] ACT 3. SCENE 2.
2 *Dra.*] *Boy.*
3 haue good] ha'good
4 *Dra.*] *Boy.*
6 *omit*; + *Boy.* Here, here, anon, anon, by and by, I come, I come. *Ex.*
7 Wthin *Ierome*] *Jerom*
13 *omit*; + *Nat.* What excellent luck had we, friend *Buzzard*, to meet with thee
17 Ist] Is it
18–19 *omit* SD
19 Here's] and her's
20–21 What dost thou sigh? There / Off] fill again boy—There, drink it off. / *Ed.* Off
22 I haue] that ere I
30 master] and master
35 fiue] two
36 *omit*; + under that *Babilonian* Tyrant *Quicksands*
40–41 & a frend / of his] to make a friend of his drink
43 I marry] I
44 *Nat.* A] A
46 himselfe dranke] drank all himself
50 night; when] night, of later memory; and I shall nere forget it, that riotous wedding night: when

56 health] full bowl
59 [+] I
+ found it before in your money when my Master (whose confusion I have drunk) took your Mortgages; And now I find it in your wine. I thank you kind gentleman still.
63 *Ed. Vin.*] *All.*
64 Gentleman borne] gentleman
65 in the] i'the
69–70 of yor Master / When he turn'd yo^{u} away. And now here's] at your ma- / sters hands, like a Gentleman, and a *Buzzard* as you / were, and he turn'd you away most beastly like / a swine, as he is. And now here is
74 I'll pledge] Ha, ha, ha. Ile pledge
75 + *Buz.* I will friend. And tother two friends, here's upon (the same.
Ed. I hope he will shew us a way, out of the bottom of his bowl to find his Mistresse.
Vin. This fellow was happily found.
76 draught. / hickvp /] draught.
77 [+] you must
+ keep no secrets amongst friends.
80 + Wee'l help thee to handle it, fear it not.
81 yee] you
82–85 *omit*; + *Vin.* What else.
Buz. Ile first take tother cup, and then out with't altogether—And now it comes—If my Mistress do bring him home a bastard, she's but even with him.
86 warrant. ha!] warrant.
88 ougliest Arsivarsiest . . . came] Arsivarsiest . . . crept
89 the wrong way into] into
93 These] this
95 A very Natrall . . . doe] Yes: A very natural; and goes a thissen . . . / do too
99 kept] kept, friend, where is he kept.
103 man] man, one Hulverhead,
104 heare more] hear
110 + *Nat.* Pray thee hold thy peace.
111 noe frend] friend, no
112 + *Nat.* Come, come; I know what we will do with / him.
113 *Nat. Mun* . . . tother] Mun . . . the other
117–20 *omit*; + *Nat.* See he jooks already. Boy shew us a private room.
Boy. This way, Gentlemen.
Buz. Down, *Plumpton-parke, &c. They lead* Buz. *out, and he sings.*

III.iv

*[This scene continues III.iii in *O*.]
1 *omit*

2 Turnd out of dores] *Arn.* Turn'd out o'doors

8–9 And / Stealing's a hanging matter. I haue noe mind to't] stealing / I have no minde to: Tis a hanging matter

10 [+ SD] *He kneels.*

12 *Nath:*] *Nat. Vin. Edm.*

13 *omit*

14 . . . at thy deuotions] *Nat.* . . . What, at thy devotion

15–27 *omit*; + *Ar.* Ile tell you in your ear, sir, I dare trust you. *Nat & Arnold whisper.*
Vi. Could earthly man have dreamt this Rascal *Quick sands.*
Whose Letchery, to all our thinking, was
Nothing but greedy Avarice and cosonage,
Could have been all this while a conceal'd whoremaster,
To have a Bastard of so many years
Nursled i'th' Countrey?
Ed. Note the punishments
That haunt the Miscreant for his black misdeeds;
That his base off-spring proves a natural Ideot;
Next that his wife, by whom he might had comfort
In progeny, though of some others getting,
Should with her light heels make him heavie-headed
By running of her Countrey! And lastly that
The blinded wretch should cast his servant off,
Who was the cover of his villany,
To shew us (that can have no mercy on him)
The way to plague him.
Vin. Ha, ha, ha— *Ed.* What do'st laugh at?
Vin. To think how nimble the poor *uzzard* is
To be reveng'd on's Master; How he has Shap'd himself;
Cut off his beard, and practis'd all the postures
To act the Changeling bastard.
Ed. Could we light
Upon some quaint old fellow now, could match him
To play the clown that brings him up to town,
Our company were full, and we were ready
To put our project into present action.
Nat. Gentlemen, we are fitted: take this man w'ye
He is the onely man I would have sought,
To give our project life. I'le trust thee *Arnold*,
And trust thou me, thou shalt get pieces by't;
Besides, Ile piece thee to thy Master again.
Ar. That clinches Sir.
Nat. Go follow your directions.
Vin. Come away then. *Ex. Vin. Ed. Arn.*

40 still.] Ha!

41 hath] has

44–45 were some deft Lasse / Or some plump Mistres] if some plump Mistriss / Or a deft Lass were

49 *omit*

50 thoughts] thought

63 Giantesse] Giants

65 Religions] Religious

70 in it] in't
73 Thou dost not thinck] But thou nere thinkst
96 [+] Tell me.
+ It shall go no further.
98 to abuse] t'abuse
99 then.] then? But I
100–2 *omit*; + Have done. And now pray speak what troubles you.
103 Then I] I
104 Town-talke shortly] Town talk
105–8 *omit*
109 *Ar.* My] My
120 i'their] in their
125 the] th'
126 a word] word
128 such] all
133 wee'll] will

III.v

*[This scene corresponds to IV.i in *O*.]
1 *Scœne. v. Enter* . . . apparraile] ACT. 4. SCENE I. . . . / *habit*
4–16 *omit*
17 *omit*; + *Dio.* Wher's the pistol you provided for me.
18 Yes: here tis] Here Mistress
19 It is too long me thincks] Tis too long
20 It would] If it were / 'Twould
21 nor . . . home else Mistres] or . . . home
22 it . . . I am] I . . . me
+ I'm sure I have often felt it.
27 + *Dio.* I dare not understand thee yet. Be sure
28 *Dio.* As] As
29 See] That
30 *omit*
31 Thou . . . I] And so thou . . . Ile
41 *omit*

IV.i

*[This scene corresponds to IV.ii in *O*.]
1 *i*] 2
2 like a black Moore] *her face black*
4 in] by
6 When those illustrious Emblemes] and shall shine forth again
7–10 *omit*

11 their] its

14 in it] in't

21 + O how I laugh to hear the cozen'd people
As I pass on the streets abuse themselves
By idle questions and false reports.
As thus: good morrow Master *Quicksands*; pray
How fares your beauteous bedfellow? says another
I hear she's not at home. A third says no:
He saw her yesterday at the still-yard
With such a Gallant, sowsing their dry'd tongues
In *Rhemish, Deal,* and *Back-rag*: Then a fourth
Sayes he knowes all her haunts and Meetings
At Bridgfoot, Bear, the Tunnes, the Cats, the Squirels;
Where, when, and in what company to find her,
But that he scornes to do poor me the favour:
Because a light piece is too good for me.
While a fifth youth with counterfeit shew of pity,
Meets, and bewails my case, and saies he knows
A Lord that must be nameless keeps my wife
In an inchanted Castle two miles West
Upon the River side: but all conclude—
Mil. That you are a monstrous cuckold, and deserve it.
Quic. Knowing my safety, then, and their foul errors,
Have I not cause to laugh? Yes, in abundance.

38–39 *omit*

44 *(Knock] A side, one / knocks* [In *O*, the SD begins on line 43.]

47 *Edmond. Vincent] Vin. Ed.*

48 for I am perswaded.] for?

54 an] a

56 pounds] pound

59 the] my

62 money] money Sir

63 *omit*

64 But . . . or would yo^{u}] *Qui.* But . . . good Sirs

65–66 *omit*

67 We . . . for] *Nat.* We . . . worth

70 I'll] We'le

75 was the likeliest] might ha'been as likely as any

76 helpe] have helpt

77 wth] withal

81 *Ed.*] *Nat.*

85 I doe purpose,] while the widowers
+ Blubber, and bath in tears (which they do seem
To wring out of their fingers ends and noses)
And after all the demure ceremony.
Are subject to be thought dissemblers, I
(To avoid the scandal of Hypocresie,

86 not me, to] me not

91 *Ed. Vin.* Yo^{u} shall haue] *Nat.* You shall ha'

92–95 *omit*

96 To morrow night yo^{u} say] *Vin.* To morrow night say you

99 *omit*; + *Nat.* We came to jear the *Jew*, and he jears us.

102 the] such
103 drift] end
108 + *Nat.* Zooks, would he had some devilish jealous hilding,
109 *Nat.* Twould] 'T would
111–12 *omit*; + Of his changeling Bastard
115 *Ed.*] *Vin.*
117 *Nat.*] *Ed.*
118 If] *Nat.* If

IV.ii

*[This scene corresponds to IV.iii in *O.*]
1 *omit*; + ACT 4. SCENE 3. / *Theophilus. Lucy.*
4 the ayre] th'air
8 speakes . . . &] speak . . . or
10 wast, in vayne, . . . timeles] waste . . . untimely
12 Yo^{u} are] y'are
13 and] if you
16 + *Lu.* So it is;
17 *Lu.* . . . part] . . . part of't
19 And] He
20 By Art, a way] A way by art
21–23 *omit*; + At least extract some drops. But do you weep
Indeed for *Millicent*? What, all these tears?
25 She was] She is
26 poore bare] empty
27 *Lu.* But] But
29 In] And
30 O how] How
36 [+SD] *Enter Page.*
37 downe good] down
40–55 *omit*
58 notes hereafter. *Ex^{t} Page.*] notes
60 very sad] sad
61 read hem S^{r}. *He reades.*] read'em.
62–64 *omit*; + *The.* They are sad indeed. How now my boy, dost weep?
I am not angry now.
68 A] He
69 Dost] Dost thou
70 Noe truly] No:
75 will . . . shall heare] that will . . . hear
77 and yo^{u} soe truly] that you so lov'd and
82 *Ent. Page &*] *Enter*
88–89 *omit*; + *The.* A lovely one he is, and wondrous like her,
98 is] were
99 + *The.* I'st not her face? you do not mind me sister.
Lu. Hers was a good one once, and this is now.
107 *omit*

111 *omit*
116 Is this] This
122 seeke them] seek'em
124 Not . . . place them] Nere . . . plant'em
125 see them] see'em
129 Sister. Here, now stand on this side] sister.
135 a kinseman, here a Stranger] allied, a stranger here
136–37 *omit*; + Yet, Sir, believe me, you in those fair eyes
Bring your own welcome with you.
139 vpon] on
144 feare if my first resolution] fear
145 *omit*

IV.iii

*[This scene corresponds to IV.iv in *O*.]
1 *Scœne. iii. Enter. Millicent. &*] ACT. 4. SCENE. 4. / *Millicent.*
13 that time, now six long twellmonths past] his traval, which is now six years
17 *omit*
20 may be] is now
24 Fy] If
28 Out of this thralldome, I] I
30–48 *omit*
49 Among the Guests, when they are come] Be sure, among the guests, that you
51 *omit*; + And then let me alone to act your *Mores* part.
53–54 *Ex^{t}. Ent Quick- / sands.*] *Enter Quic. / Exit. Phi.* [In *O*, the SD begins at line 52.]
58 houre S^{r}] hour
59 base obscuritie] obscurity.
61 of them] of'em
64 much sad of late] late posses'd with sadnes
65 + To be partaker more of your mirth then chear.
67 *omit*
68 *Nat.* Ha'yo^{u}] Ha'you
72 not I] I ha'sworn
73 *omit*
74–75 *omit*; + *Ar.* You were too rash, Sir, in that oath, if I
May be allowed to speak.
81 none] none, nor you if you speak so.
82 Nay, I haue] Sir, *I* ha'
83–84 *omit*
85 *Nat*] *Nat.* It is
86 euer] ere
89 see] see, Sir,
91 S^{r}] how
+ *Art.* Will you have dancing here to night.

Quic. Yes I have borrowed other *Moors* of Merchants
That trade in *Barbary*, whence I had mine own here,
And you shall see their way and skill in dancing.

92 white] white white
+ With confidence none will cheat him of a bit;
96 sparckling] sparklingst
98 on fire] a fire
99 *omit*; + And the keel mourning, (how I shall rejoyce
At these prepostrous splendours) get thee glorious;
102 meet] clap
109 pax] pox
110 the fine-a whit-a Gentillman-a] de fine white Zentilmanna
115 more-a *Ext.*] more a.
116 thee for more-a then I'll] the Moor-a for more then I / Will
118 In *O*, the SD occurs at line 119.
122 hah s^{r} hah] hah
125–27 *omit*
128 . . . *(whisper)*] *Quic.* . . .
129–31 *omit*; + You shall have instantly an entertainment, that
132 To] Shall
138 conscious] guilty
141 thee] you
143 the] that the
145 Betwixt] Between
147–48 *omit*
149 Yo^{r}selfe] And you
152–53 *omit*; + *Tes.* Pray what have you been to her? I nere found you
158 in] and in
160 but] and
165 haue yo^{u} . . . *Edmond.*] ha'you . . . *&* / *Edm.*
166 wyee] with you
167 o^{r}] and our
169 on foot; a shew of *Blackamores*] a foot. Here's Revels towards.
+ *Ed.* A daunce of furies or of Blackamores
Is practising within;
Vin. But first there is to be some odd collation
In stead of supper.
Nat. Cheap enough I warrant,
170 *Nat.* But . . . among hem] But . . . amongst'em
171–74 *omit*; + *Ed.* A pretty little Rogue, most richly deck'd
175 *Ed.* Wth . . . Shee's the] With . . . She is
179 *Vin.*] *Ed.*
180 weares] wears. But mum my Masters
186 *Nat. Vinc. Edm*] 3
187–89 *omit*; + *Tes.* If she does live (as he bears me in hand
She is not dead) Ile tell you briefly, Sir,
200–202 [SD] *omit*; + Exit, Enter
Mili. white-
fac'd & in her
ovvn habit.
[In *O*, the SD begins at line 198.]
203 peace . . . meeke] self . . . milde

206 illuminated] illumin'd
227–29 *omit*
230 What's] *Ar.* What's
236 quickly] quickly*:* why do you stoop?
245 professe most fairly.] profess—
247 till I] and not

IV.iv

*[This scene corresponds to IV.v in *O.*]
1 *Scœne iiii.*] ACT 4. SCENE 5.
6 Wth] And
7 Yo^{u} haue . . . shall yo^{u}] Y'have . . . you shall
8 restore] return
9 *omit*; + *Vin.* I hope he'l marry his Moor to anger us.
10 giue him] give her
11 And] And't
11–15 [SD] *omit*; + Florish *enter*
Inductor
like a Moor
leading Phil-
lis (*black*
and) *gorge-*
ously deck't
with jewels.
14 *Actor.*] *Ind.*
17 *Actor.*] *Ind.*
20 *Actor.*] *Ind.*
+ *Tes.* He puts the blockheads on'hem grosly.
Quic. Brave impudent rogue. He made the speeches last (year
Before my Lord Marquess of *Fleet* Conduit.
21 . . . feares] *Ind.* . . . fear
26–28 *omit*
31 to married] married to
33 *Ed.*] *Vin.*
34 as white] white
35 *Act.*] *Ind.*
41 *Act.*] *Ind.* [+SD] *He looks in* Ed- / monds *hand.*
43 *Act.*] *Ind.*
47 *Act.*] *Ind.* [+SD] *In* Vin. *his / hand.*
48 Liues] lifes
49 that made] made
53 hang'd] hung
55 *omit*; + *Ind.* Nor you, sir: For *In* Nats *hand.*
58 I would] Would
59 *Act.*] *Ind.*

60 [+SD] *In Quic. hand*

62–65 *omit*; + *Enter the rest of the Moors. They Dance an Antique in which they use action of Mockery and derision to the three Gentlemen.*

Nat. We applaud your devise, and you'l give me leave
To take your black bride here, forth in a daunce.

67 *omit*; + *Nat.* Musick, play a Galliard,
You know what you promised me, *Bullis*.

70 Play] *Nat.* Play

71 yo^{u}'ll] will you

72 my a] my

73–74 *omit*

74–75 [SD] *omit*; + *Nat. daunces vily. Quicks. & Tes. laughs & looks off.*

[In *O*, the SD begins at line 72.]

75 Soe] *Nat.* So

77–83 [SD] *omit*; + *Enter* Arnold *like a Countrey man, and* Buz. *like a changling, and as they enter, exit* Nat. *with* Phil. *the Musick still playing.*

81 braue o braue o braue] brave, o brave

85–86 *omit*; + *Buz.* Hack ye there, hack ye there,
O brave pipes. Hack ye there.
Hey toodle loodle loodle loo.
He sings and dances and spins with a Rock & spindle.

87 yee] you

88 and] if

89 man S^{r}.] man

91 [+SD] *Softly.*

92 then ta] it

95 child of yo^{r}s. Say yo^{u}] simple child of yours

96 I say thou knowst not what thou sayst. I] I

98 and I'll] Ile

101 those] these

102–4 *omit* SD

103 O deuilish mischiefe. Get] Get

104 came] come

105 in] of

107 Besworne] I swear

109 Yes, tell] Tell

112 me of a chardge that lies vpon my hands] my self of a charge

113 Of] off

115 ouer much asham'd] asham'd

116 graue] grave and wise

118 Hay] with a Hay

121 doe . . . bastards] does . . . children
+ *Buz.* With a hay toodle loodle loodle loo, &c.

122 then marry] marry

124 *Ed.*] *Vin.*
125 + *Arn.* He needs none o'your skill it seems.
126 loodle looe] &c
128 am content to . . . open to] will . . . before
129–33 *omit*; + For a poor servant that I had, I undertook and paid
For keeping of an ideot.
Ed. Who, your man *Buzzard*?
Qui. Even he.
Buz. Hay toodle loodle, &c.
Qui. 'Tis like this is the child. But for a certain sum
Which I did pay, 'twas articled, that I should nere be
Troubled with it more.
136 he is now become] now he is
137 *Ed.*] *Vin.* [+SD] *Buzzard / spinns.*
138 *omit*
146 ferkt] fetch'd
148 looe.] &c.
150 it] here it
151 *Vin.*] *Ed.*
153 sha'nt . . . allthough ta] sha'not . . . though it
155–56 (Thanck yo^{u} for yor good will / How euer Gentleman)]
I am none of his hirelings, nor / His Tenants I.
158 moreouer] you / May know
165 *Ed.*] *Vin.*
167 *omit*
170 *Ed.* Because] because
171 vpon] on
174 *Vin.*] *Ed.*
175 *Ed.*] *Vin.*
180 a knees. Ah—ah.] my knees. A—ah. Hay
181 yee] you
182 *Moore-actor*] *Moors*
183 yo^{u}] you, ye Rascals
184 *Actor.*] *Moor.*
185 Service] true service
186 not to] we will not
189 *Actor.*] *Moor.*
190 here] Sir
193 *Act:* . . . what] *Moor.* . . . which
194 [+] made this same a baudy house;
+ How will you have it?
198 liuing man] man on earth
199 speakst] speakest
200 + *Buz.* Hay toodle loodle, &c.
203 *Omnes.* How!] *All.* How Sir
+ *Ed.* In conceit you mean.
204 My] I say my
208 in] before a Court in
210–11 *omit*; + Friends, guard the doors. None shall depart the house.
212 *Vin. Ed.* Good S^{r}] *Mun. Vin.* Content,
213 + *Qui.* Oh—
214 yee] you

217–21 *omit*; + *Tes.* You know your Chamber huswife. I'le wait o'your (Master
To night. We will not part until to morrow day,
223 the merry night] your merry night, Sir
224 oh—oh—] oh—oh—o—
228 *omit*; + *Qui.* Oh o—*Buz.* Hay toodle loodle, &c. / *Exeunt omnes.*
229 *omit*

V.i

5 *omit*
7 Will giue a true] We'le render a
15 land but that] sand but theirs
24 there? ah ha!] there?
25 riming] running
27 my] the
37 the Compter] th'Compters
38 doffing a false] pulling off a
41 take them] take'em
42 ran] runs
44 nor yet, nor yet] nor yet
45 worst] bad
46 you haue] y'have
50 *omit*
51 For] In
54 six yeares bene] been six years
68 Rime] ruine
78 Heare one, (I make noe doubt)] (I make no doubt) here one
81 flesh] flesh, do you hear?
82–83 *omit*; + *Rash.* Why dost thou tell him this?
85 the fouler] that wicked
86 is it?] is't?
89 was] has
91 haue scap'd] scape
96 + *Host.* Sir, Ile tell you.
97 *Host.* I haue in the house] I have, i'th'house
98 *omit*
99 *Host.* Yes Sr, and . . . ouer] And . . . ore I'm sure on't
103 Pray thee to the point] But to the point, I pray thee
105 in the house] i'th'house
106 Sometimes he spends] Spending
107 And most] Most
+ And who loves who, and who keeps home, and so forth;
108 told you] tell you
109 In *O*, the SD occurs at line 110.
111 Nay] Nay, nay,
113 killd him] he kil'd
119 (By what I heare), or] Or

120 soe the deuill haue] the Devil / Have so
122 What is] Whats
127 might] and
129 *Oẽs.*] *All.*
131 to beget delay. Yo^{r}] in delay; your sudden
133 me] my
134 yo^{u}] ye
135 *Ras. Mean.* Goe wee'll] *Rash.* Go, we

V.ii

1 *omit*; + ACT. 5. SCENE 2. / *Dionysia as before in mans habit, sword and pistol.*
11 thy Liege-right] the liege-right
19 *Lucy*] *& Lucy*
20 to yo^{u}] you
23–24 *omit*
25–29 [SD] *omit*; + *Ent. Ar. in his false beard, leading in Mil. veil'd. Pages they stand a-loofe.*
[In *O*, the SD begins at line 22.]
29 gentleman is that her arme's] young Gentleman is that your Mistris / (arm / Appears
30 name] name, as you said, neither.
+ *Ar.* He seems some well grac'd suitor. 'Tis my fear,
If he should now—I must be just however.
31 S^{r}, here's] *Pa.* Sir,
35–36 *omit*
37 *The.* That] O'tis the
38 sister, yet vnkowne] Sister:
43 to inquire] t'enquire
45 though] if
49 Euer can] Can ever
56 willfully] willingly
61 to] for
62 tis . . . *Ex*] it is . . .
69–74 *omit*
75 + I shall be straight discover'd too. False Love
76 Loue thou hast dealt falsely] Thou hast dealt loosely
77 [+] Now
\+ Possesse me wholly; let it not be thought
I came and went off idly.
Lu. Sir, something troubles you. See your kinswoman
My brother stands intranc'd too; Brother, brother—
78 *Lu.* Brother, how stand yo^{u}? Noble] Noble
80 *Lu.* . . . I feare, hath cras'd him] . . . transmutes him—Sir,
81 *Mil.* S^{r}, be not] Be not so
96–98 *omit*; + I can resolve you all; but for the present

He will be known to none.

103 subtle things] subtle

104–7 *omit*; + *Mil.* This was my fear. Will you have patience,
And sit but in this chair while I relate my story.

109–11 *omit* SD

113–16 [SD] *omit*; + *As* Dionisia
presents her
pistol. Enter
Rash. Mean.
Win. Rafe.
Arthur.

119 Hold fast the Murderesse.] Stay the murdress there.

119–20 *omit* SD

120 *omit*; + I suspect your son too / Is not without a hand in't

121 great hast . . . in from hence] hast . . . in

125–26 *omit*

127 Looke] *Rash.* Look

128 we all are in *Elizium* then] w'are all then in *Elisium*

132 thinck vs] see

134 yo^{u}] ye

145 health] life

147 let] Sir, let

150 yo^{u}] ye

154–55 *omit*

156 Now, how dos he] How does he now

158 pray; And m^{r} *Winlosse*] pray.

159 *omit*

160 *omit*; + *Ar. &c.* He shall have all our cares.

160–62 [SD] *omit*; + *Exit with* The. / *in the chair.*

162 for] to

165 *Ex^{t} Amb*] *Exit*

V.iii

1 *omit*; + ACT. 5. SCENE 3. / *Vincent. Edmond. Testy. Rashly. Meanwel.*

2–23 *omit*; + *Vin.* Come, we will hear this cause try'd.
Ed. See the judges
Have tane their seats, while we stand here for evidence.

24 *omit* SD

27 But to] To

30 place here of] chief place in

33 *Rash.* Yo^{r}] Your [In *O*, lines 32 and 33 are reversed.]

34 *omit*

35 yo^{u}] we

36 first beginne noe new ones] begin no new one first

37 I haue] Sir, I ha'
+ *Mea.* Pray Sir fall to the question.
Test. Bring in the parties. Ent. *Quic.* / *Nat. Phil.*

38 [*Tes.*] The] The

39 Whether] If

40 (Bring in the parties). Speake yo^{u} Gentlemen.] Speak Gentlemen. What can you say to this?

41 He did affirme] *Quicksands* affirm'd

42–44 In *O*, the SD occurs after line 37. See above.

46 *Moore*] Moor, there

48 Still it] That same

60 faire] firm

62 my Neece is irrevocable] is irrecoverable

64 euer] ere

65 shee is] she's

77 *omit*

82 lewd] leane

86 Hoping yet] Hoping

87 all shee beares] all

103 me. I'll nippe thee dead else] me.

104 *omit*

105 Sir, Sir] Sirrah

109 *Rash.*] *Tes.*

110 [+] Answer me, where is she?

111 *omit*

115 *omit*

116 Murdrer, speake] Murderer

120 Shee's thought to] If she must

123 mine] my

124 yo^{u}] we

125 haue bene soe wth me] know

126 though] because

128 yo^{u} haue] y'have

131 Shall] To

134 *omit*

135–38 [SD] *omit*; + Ent. *The. Mil.*
Ar. Lu. Dio.
Winloss.

144 vast] past

146 I would] Ile

151 shall] will

156 of their] o'their

160 *omit*; + *Nat.* That's well agen.
Phi. It was but in attempt, I told my Mistriss,
Had it been done, sure I should nere have spoke on't.
Nat. Those are the councels women can onely keep.
Phi. Nothing in act I assure you.

161 *Nat.*] *Mil.*

164 the example. Where's his bastard?] for proof his bastard there.

165–66 *Arnold* / *Buzzard*] *Buz.* / *Arn.*

166 it] the lash

169 *play*] *come play*

170 *omit* SD

174 We] *Ed.* We

177 *Ed.*] *Vin.*

178 forfeit Mortgages] mortgages

180 goodly beard he wore, for] beard he wore; for loss of

181 *omit*; + We'le recompence him.

188 away] away so

189 Come] Ha, ha, ha. Come

194 that . . . to his] too . . . to's

198 her] ye

204 + (By making man, and the world meer strangers to me,

209 now, m^{r} *Banelasse*! Doe yo^{u} looke squeamishly] now! do you look squemish

210 Vpon] on

212 defild it Tis good yo^{u} purify't] defile it, / Tis best you cleanse it

213 will. pray Giue her S^{r} yor blessing.] will—

214 *omit*

215 *omit*; + Forgiv'me for swearing, and turn Precisian,

216 pray . . . speed noe better] pray / I'the nose . . . whoremasters spend no / (worse

221 thee. I bobd too much before] thee

222 All pleasd I hope] I hope all pleas'd

224 *Epilogue. I*] I

226 *omit*; + EPILOGUE.

NOw let me be a modest undertaker
For us the players, the play and the play-maker:
If we have faild in speech or Action, we
Must crave a pardon; If the Commedy
Either in mirth, or matter be not right,
As'twas intended unto your delight,
The Poet in hope of favour doth submit
Unto your censure both himself and it,
Wishing that as y'are judges in the cause
You judge but by the antient Comick Lawes.
Not by their course who in this latter age
Have sown such pleasing errors on the stage,
Which he no more will chuse to imitate
Then they to fly from truth, and run the State.
But whether I avail, you have seen the play,
And all that in defence the Poet can say
Is, that he cannot mend it by a jest
I'th Epilogue exceeding all the rest;
To send you off upon a champing bit,
More then the scenes afforded of his wit:
Nor studies he the Art to have it said
He sculks behind the hangings as affraid
Of a hard censure, or pretend to brag
Here's all your money again brought in i'th bag
If you applaud not, when before the word
'Twas parcel'd out upon the shearing-board [sharing-board].
Such are fine helps; but are not practised yet
By our plain Poet who cannot forget
His wonted modesty, and humble way
For him and us, and his yet doubtful play,
Which, if receiv'd or but allow'd by you,
We and the play are yours, the Poet too.

Bibliography

Adams, Joseph Quincy, ed. *The Dramatic Records of Sir Henry Herbert, Master of the Revels, 1623–1673*. New Haven: Yale University Press, 1917.

———. "Hill's List of Early Plays in Manuscript." *Library*, 4th ser., vol. 20 (1939): 71–99.

Albright, Evelyn May. *Dramatic Publication in England, 1580–1640: A Study of Conditions Affecting Content and Form of Drama*. New York: MLA, 1927.

Andrews, Clarence E. *Richard Brome: A Study of His Life and Works*. Yale Studies in English, vol. 46. New York: Henry Holt, 1913.

Arber, Edward, ed. *A Transcript of the Registers of the Company of Stationers of London, 1554–1640 A.D.* Vol. 4. 1877. Reprint. New York: Peter Smith, 1950.

Armstrong, William A. "The Audience of the Elizabethan Private Theatres." *Review of English Studies*, n.s. 10 (1959): 234–49.

Ashley, Maurice. *Life in Stuart England*. London: Batsford; New York: Putnam, 1964.

———. "Love and Marriage in Seventeenth-Century England." *History Today* 8 (1958): 667–75.

Aylmer, G. E. *The King's Servants: The Civil Service of Charles I, 1625–1642*. London: Routledge; New York: Columbia University Press, 1961.

Bayne, Ronald. "Lesser Jacobean and Caroline Dramatists." In *The Cambridge History of English Literature*, edited by A. W. Ward and A. R. Waller, vol. 6:210–40. 1910. Reprint. London: Cambridge University Press, 1919.

Benedikz, B. S. Letter to author, 24 October 1977.

———, comp. *Lichfield Cathedral Library: An Interim Catalogue of the Cathedral Manuscripts*. 1974.

Bentley, Gerald Eades. *The Jacobean and Caroline Stage*. 7 vols. Oxford: Clarendon, 1941–1968.

———. *The Profession of Dramatist in Shakespeare's Time, 1590–1642*. Princeton: Princeton University Press, 1971.

———, ed. *The Seventeenth-Century Stage: A Collection of Critical Essays*. Chicago: University of Chicago Press, 1968.

Blaxton, John. *The English Usurer, or, Usury Condemned*. 1634. Reprint. Norwood, N.J.: Walter J. Johnson, 1974.

Blayney, Glenn H. "Enforcement of Marriage in English Drama (1600–1650)." *Philological Quarterly* 38 (1959): 459–72.

Boswell, Eleanore, and E. K. Chambers, eds. "Dramatic Records: The Lord Chamberlain's Office." In vol. 2, pt. 3 of *Malone Society Collections*, edited by W. W. Greg, 321–416. Oxford: Oxford University Press, 1931.

Bowden, William R. *The English Dramatic Lyric, 1603–42: A Study in Stuart Dramatic Technique*. New Haven: Yale University Press, 1951.

Brewer, Ebenezer Cobham. *Dictionary of Phrase and Fable*. Rev. ed. Edited by Ivor H. Evans. New York: Harper & Row, 1970.

Briquet, C. M. *Les Filigranes: Dictionnaire historique des marques du papier dès leur apparition vers 1282 jusqu'en 1600*. Edited by Allan Stevenson. 1907. Reprint. Amsterdam: Paper Publications Society, 1968.

Brome, Richard. *The Dramatic Works of Richard Brome Containing Fifteen Comedies Now First Collected in Three Volumes*. 3 vols. London: John Pearson, 1873.

———. *The Dramatic Works of Richard Brome Containing Fifteen Comedies Now First Collected in Three Volumes*. 3 vols. 1873. Reprint. New York: AMS Press, 1966.

———. *The English Moor*. In his *Five New Playes*, 1–84. London: A. Crooke & H. Brome, 1659.

———. *The English Moore*. MS. 68. Lichfield Cathedral Library, Lichfield, England.

———. *The English Moor*. Typescript. In W. G. Hergest, Master's thesis, University of London, 1928.

———. *Five New Playes*. London: A. Crooke & H. Brome, 1659.

[———?] "Praeludium for Thomas Goffe's *The Careless Shepherdess* (c. 1638)." In *The Seventeenth-Century Stage: A Collection of Critical Essays*, edited by Gerald Eades Bentley, 28–37. Chicago: University of Chicago Press, 1968.

———. "To the Memory of the Deceased, but Ever-Living Author in These his Poems, Master John Fletcher." In vol. 1 of *The Works of Beaumont and Fletcher*, edited by Alexander Dyce, 63–65. London: Moxon, 1843.

———, ed. *Lachrymae Musarum: The Tears of the Muses*. London: Tho. Newcomb, 1649.

Camden, Carroll. *The Elizabethan Woman*. Houston and New York: Elsevier, 1952.

Chappell, William, ed. *The Roxburghe Ballads*. Vol. 1. 1869. Reprint. New York: AMS Press, 1966.

Churchill, W[illiam] A. *Watermarks in Paper in Holland, England, France, Etc., in the XVII and XVIII Centuries and Their Interconnection*. 1935. Reprint. Meppel, Netherlands: Krips Reprint, 1967.

Cope, Jackson I. *The Theater and the Dream: From Metaphor to Form in Renaissance Drama*. Baltimore: Johns Hopkins University Press, 1973.

Cutts, John. "The Anonymous Masque-Like Entertainment in Egerton MS. 1994, and Richard Brome." *Comparative Drama* 1 (1967): 277–87.

Davis, Joe Lee. *The Sons of Ben: Jonsonian Comedy in Caroline England*. Detroit: Wayne State University Press, 1967.

Eliot, T. S. "Imperfect Critics: Swinburne as Critic." In his *Sacred Wood: Essays on Poetry and Criticism*. 3d ed., 17–24. London: Methuen, 1932.

Fleay, Frederick G. *A Biographical Chronicle of the English Drama, 1559–1642*. 1891. Reprint. New York: Burt Franklin, 1962.

Freehafer, John. "Perspective Scenery and the Caroline Playhouses." *Theatre Notebook* 27 (1973): 98–113.

Greg, W. W. *A Bibliography of the English Printed Drama to the Restoration*. Vol. 2. London: Oxford University Press, 1951.

Guardia, Charles E. "Richard Brome as a Follower of Ben Jonson." Master's thesis, Louisiana State University, 1938.

Haaker, Ann. Letter to James L. Harner, 24 July 1978.

———. "The Plague, the Theater, and the Poet." *Renaissance Drama*, n.s. 1 (1968): 283–306.

Hamilton, William Douglas, ed. *Calendar of State Papers, Domestic, Charles I*. Vol. 18. London: Eyre & Spottiswoode, 1887.

Harbage, Alfred. *Cavalier Drama: An Historical and Critical Supplement to the Study of the Elizabethan and the Restoration Stage*. 1936. Reprint. New York: Russell & Russell, 1964.

Hazlitt, W. C[arew], ed. *The English Drama and Stage under the Tudor and Stuart Princes, 1543–1664, Illustrated by a Series of Documents, Treatises, and Poems*, 253–58. 1869. Reprint. New York: Burt Franklin, n.d.

———, ed. *Inedited Tracts: Illustrating the Manners, Opinions, and Occupations of*

Englishmen During the Sixteenth and Seventeenth Centuries. 1868. Reprint. New York: Burt Franklin, 1964.

Ingram, R. W. "The Musical Art of Richard Brome's Comedies." *Renaissance Drama*, n.s. 7 (1958): 219–42.

Jefferson, Richard. "Some Aspects of Richard Brome's Comedies of Manners: A Re-Interpretation." Ph.D. diss., University of Wisconsin, 1955.

Jones, Eldred D. *The Elizabethan Image of Africa*. [Charlottesville]: University Press of Virginia, 1971.

———. "The Physical Representation of African Characters on the English Stage During the 16th and 17th Centuries." *Theatre Notebook* 17 (1962): 17–21.

Jonson, Ben. *Ben Jonson*. Edited by C. H. Herford, Percy Simpson, and Evelyn Simpson. 11 vols. Oxford: Clarendon, 1925–1952.

Kaufmann, R[alph] J. *Richard Brome: Caroline Playwright*. New York: Columbia University Press, 1961.

Kiehl, Ellen Dutton. "The Comedy of Richard Brome: A Study of Comic Form and Function." Ph.D. diss., State University of New York at Albany, 1977.

Lichfield Cathedral Library: A Catalogue of the Printed Books and Manuscripts in the Library of the Cathedral Church of Lichfield. London: Sotheran; Lichfield: Lomax, 1888.

Marmion, Shakerly. *A Fine Companion* [1633]. In *The Dramatic Works of Shackerley Marmion*. London: Sotheran, 1875.

Middleton, Thomas, and William Rowley. *The Changeling*. Edited by George Walton Williams. Regents Renaissance Drama Series. Lincoln: University of Nebraska Press, 1966.

Onions, C[harles] T. *A Shakespeare Glossary*. Rev. ed., 1958. Reprint. Oxford: Clarendon, 1966.

Partridge, Eric. *Shakespeare's Bawdy: A Literary & Psychological Essay and a Comprehensive Glossary*. 1948. Reprint. New York: Dutton, 1960.

Petti, Anthony G. *English Literary Hands from Chaucer to Dryden*. Cambridge: Harvard University Press, 1977.

Plomer, Henry R. *A Dictionary of the Booksellers and Printers Who were at Work in England, Scotland and Ireland from 1641 to 1667*. London: Blades, East & Blades, 1907.

Rigg, James McMullen. "Seymour, William," [1917]. *DNB*.

Seymour, Frances, Duchess of Somerset. Will. Public Records Office. Wills Division. Probate 355, fol. 133.

Shaw, Catherine Maud. "The Dramatic Function of the Masque in English Drama, 1592–1642." Ph.D. diss., University of Texas, 1967.

———. *Richard Brome*. Twayne English Authors Series. Boston: G. K. Hall, 1980.

Simpson, Claude M. *The British Broadside Ballad and Its Music*. New Brunswick: Rutgers University Press, 1966.

Skeat, Walter W. *A Glossary of Tudor and Stuart Words, Especially from the Dramatists*. Edited by A. L. Mayhew. 1914. Reprint. New York: Burt Franklin, 1968.

Smith, G. C. Moore. "The Canon of Randolph's Dramatic Works." *Review of English Studies* 1 (1925): 309–23.

The Stage-Players Complaint: In a Pleasant Dialogue betweene Cane of the Fortune, and Reed of the Friers [1641]. In *The English Drama and Stage under the Tudor and Stuart Princes, 1543–1664, Illustrated by a Series of Documents, Treatises, and Poems*, edited by W. C[arew] Hazlitt, 253–58. 1869. Reprint. New York: Burt Franklin, n.d.

Stonex, Arthur B. "The Usurer in Elizabethan Drama." *PMLA* 31 (1916): 190–210.

Sugden, Edward H. *A Topographical Dictionary to the Works of Shakespeare and His Fellow Dramatists*. Manchester: Manchester University Press, 1925.

Swinburne, Algernon Charles. "Richard Brome." *Fortnightly* 304 (1892): 500–507.

Thaler, Alwin. "Was Richard Brome an Actor?" *Modern Language Notes* 36 (1921): 88–91.

Tilley, Morris Palmer. *A Dictionary of the Proverbs in England in the Sixteenth and Seventeenth Centuries: A Collection of the Proverbs Found in English Literature and the Dictionaries of the Period*. Ann Arbor: University of Michigan Press, 1950.

Tokson, Elliot Harvey. "The Popular Image of the Black Man in English Drama, 1550–1688." Ph.D. diss., Columbia University, 1970.

Wagner, Bernard M. "Manuscript Plays of the Seventeenth Century." *Times Literary Supplement*, 4 October 1934, 675.

Wallace, Charles William. "Shakspere and the Blackfriars." *Century* 80 (1910): 742–52.

Ward, Adolphus William. *A History of English Dramatic Literature to the Death of Queen Anne*. Vol. 2. London: Macmillan, 1875.

Webb, Margaret A. K. "Richard Brome, Caroline Dramatist: A Study of Brome's Development as a Playwright." Ph.D. diss., University of California at Berkeley, 1972.

Wilson, Thomas. *A Discourse upon Usury* [1572]. Edited by R. H. Tawney. 1925. Reprint. New York: Kelley, 1965.

Wilson, Violet A. *Society Women of Shakespeare's Time*. 1924. Reprint. Port Washington, N.Y.: Kennikat, 1970.

Wright, Celeste T. "Some Conventions Regarding the Usurer in Elizabethan Literature." *Studies in Philology* 31 (1934): 176–97.

———. "The Usurer's Sin in Elizabethan Literature." *Studies in Philology* 35 (1938): 178–94.

Wright, Joseph. *The English Dialect Dictionary*. 6 vols. London: Frowde, 1898–1905.

Index